# Freddie Prinze, Jr.

# TITLES IN THE
# LATINO BIOGRAPHY LIBRARY SERIES:

## César Chávez
### A Voice for Farmworkers
ISBN-13: 978-0-7660-2489-2
ISBN-10: 0-7660-2489-X

## Diego Rivera
### Legendary Mexican Painter
ISBN-13: 978-0-7660-2486-1
ISBN-10: 0-7660-2486-5

## Freddie Prinze, Jr.
### From Shy Guy to Movie Star
ISBN-13: 978-0-7660-2965-1
ISBN-10: 0-7660-2965-4

## Frida Kahlo
### Her Life in Paintings
ISBN-13: 978-0-7660-2487-8
ISBN-10: 0-7660-2487-3

## George Lopez
### Latino King of Comedy
ISBN-13: 978-0-7660-2968-2
ISBN-10: 0-7660-2968-9

## Gloria Estefan
### Superstar of Song
ISBN-13: 978-0-7660-2490-8
ISBN-10: 0-7660-2490-3

## Isabel Allende
### Award-Winning Latin American Author
ISBN-13: 978-0-7660-2488-5
ISBN-10: 0-7660-2488-1

## Pablo Neruda
### Passion, Poetry, Politics
ISBN-13: 978-0-7660-2966-8
ISBN-10: 0-7660-2966-2

## Jaime Escalante
### Inspirational Math Teacher
ISBN-13: 978-0-7660-2967-5
ISBN-10: 0-7660-2967-0

## Roberto Clemente
### Baseball Legend
ISBN-13: 978-0-7660-2485-4
ISBN-10: 0-7660-2485-7

# Freddie Prinze, Jr.

## From Shy Guy to Movie Star

## SALLY LEE

 **Enslow Publishers, Inc.**
40 Industrial Road
Box 398
Berkeley Heights, NJ 07922
USA
http://www.enslow.com

**Library of Congress Cataloging-in-Publication Data**

Lee, Sally.
    Freddie Prinze, Jr. : from shy guy to movie star / Sally Lee.
      p. cm. — (Latino biography library)
    Includes bibliographical references and index.
    Summary: "A biography of actor Freddie Prinze, Jr., that discusses his childhood, struggle for success, family life, and his many acting achievements in movies and on television"—Provided by publisher.
    ISBN-13: 978-0-7660-2965-1
    ISBN-10: 0-7660-2965-4
    1. Prinze, Freddie, Jr. 2. Actors—United States—Biography—Juvenile literature. 3. Hispanic American actors—Biography—Juvenile literature. I. Title.
    PN2287.P714L44 2009
    791.4302'8092—dc22
    [B]              2007046737

Printed in the United States of America

10 9 8 7 6 5 4 3 2 1

**Illustration Credits:** Associated Press, pp. 16, 102–103; Everett Collection, pp. 5, 57, 60, 65, 69, 88; Getty Images, pp. 6, 46; © Greengrass Productions/Courtesy: Everett Collection, p. 38; © Miramax Films/Courtesy: Everett Collection, p. 49; Photo by Peter Brooker/Courtesy Everett Collection, p. 74; Photofest, pp. 3, 10, 15, 25, 81, 99; © Prisma/SuperStock, p. 91; © Sony Pictures/Courtesy: Everett Collection, p. 41; Shutterstock.com, Cary Kalscheuer, p. 33; Shutterstock.com, Joseph, pp. 27.

**Cover Illustration:** Photofest.

# Contents

Actor Freddie Prinze, Jr., makes an appearance on MTV's *Total Request Live* on January 6, 2006, in New York City.

# 1

# A New Star on the Horizon

In the fall of 1994, Freddie Prinze, Jr., arrived in Hollywood. The eighteen-year-old faced a tremendous challenge. He was just one of thousands of talented actors flocking to the movie capital in search of stardom. They all shared the dream of becoming one of Hollywood's success stories. Very few of them would ever reach the level of fame they desired.

In many ways, the odds were against Prinze. At eighteen, he was younger than most of his competitors. He lacked the training many hopeful actors received from colleges or theatrical schools. Unlike those who had spent years sharpening their skills in college productions, he had little formal acting experience.

Prinze did have several things going for him. The tall, clean-cut young man with the soulful dark eyes was certainly handsome enough to be a movie star. He shared the name of his famous father, a successful

## Stiff Competition

The road to stardom is difficult. Actors face stiff competition for the limited number of starring roles available. It is even harder for the young hopefuls who often lack experience and formal training. They must compete against more seasoned actors. Many give up when they see that acting is not the quick path to fame and fortune they expected.

Very few actors become major stars. There are over one hundred twenty thousand members of the Screen Actors Guild (SAG), the union for people working in films, television, and other media. According to the *Occupational Outlook Handbook* from the Bureau of Labor Statistics, only about fifty of them could be considered highly paid stars. The average amount SAG members earn through their acting is less than five thousand dollars a year. That is because acting jobs do not come up that often.

Breaking into show business requires hard work, patience, determination, and a lot of luck. Whenever a young actor breaks the barrier and becomes a star, it is truly an event to celebrate.

comedian and television star. Although Prinze's father had died seventeen years earlier, many people in show business still remembered him. But most of all, Prinze had determination and a dream he refused to give up on.

Although Prinze would have loved to become a star instantly, he knew it was going to take a long time. He spent his first five years in Hollywood taking acting classes and studying with acting coaches. He gained experience in small roles on television and in low-budget independent films. Prinze became more recognized after appearing in two popular teen horror films. His career was progressing nicely, but at that point, no one considered him a star.

That changed on Friday, January 29, 1999, with the opening of *She's All That*. The date already had a special meaning for Prinze. It marked the twenty-second anniversary of his father's death. In January 1977, Freddie Prinze, Sr., shot himself while under the influence of prescription drugs. He was only twenty-two at the time.

Prinze, Jr., was now twenty-two years old himself. At first, the date chosen for his movie's release startled him. "I was like, 'What?! Is this some kind of sick joke?'" he said. Later he felt that it was fitting for it to open on that date, calling the coincidence "kind of trippy."[1]

The date turned out to be lucky for Prinze. *She's All That* was an instant success. It was number one at the box office, earning more than any other film shown that weekend. It brought in $16 million in just a few days

**Freddie Prinze, Jr., and Rachael Leigh Cook star in *She's All That.***

and stayed in the top five movies for several weeks. No other Miramax film had reached that level. The movie's success was especially unusual for a film aimed at the teen market. *She's All That*, which had cost $10 million to make, eventually brought in over $63 million just in the United States. Worldwide, the movie earned over $103 million.[2]

In Prinze's first leading movie role, he plays Zach, a popular high school senior. Zach is humiliated when his girlfriend publicly dumps him. In a weak moment, he bets his friends that he can turn any girl into a prom queen in two weeks. His friends pick Laney Boggs, a darkly serious artist played by Rachael Leigh Cook. The growth of their unlikely relationship brings big changes to both characters.

Prinze's life changed as soon as *She's All That* was released. He was suddenly thrust into the spotlight. Teens chose him as the latest heartthrob, and fans idolized him. Photographers pursued him. His face appeared on the covers of many fan magazines.

Being hounded by admirers was flattering, but Prinze was uncomfortable with all the attention. "I get kind of like claustrophobic," he admitted. "So it gets a little creepy, but I just try to do my thing and stay nice to everybody, and make sure they know that I do appreciate it, because I don't want people to mistake fear for rudeness."[3]

For the first time in his life, Prinze had to reschedule his activities so as not to attract too much attention. Before he became famous, he and his friends played miniature golf on Friday nights. They had to start playing on weekdays to avoid the crowds.

The success of *She's All That* put Prinze on the receiving end of several awards. He won three Fox/*Seventeen* Teen Choice Awards at the 1999 show. His fans picked him for "Choice Actor in a Film" and "Male Hottie of the Year." Prinze and Cook shared the award for "Best Love Scene." The Teen Choice Awards were especially

> **"I think of making movies as a team effort, and sometimes you are the quarterback and sometimes you are the receiver."**

meaningful to Prinze because they were voted on by the teens themselves.

Prinze was also proud to be honored for his Latino heritage. He was nominated for an American Latino Media Arts (ALMA) award. ALMA awards go to performers and musicians who depict Latinos in a positive way. *She's All That* brought him a nomination for "Outstanding Actor in a Feature Film." It was his second nomination by ALMA. In 1999, Prinze had been nominated for "Outstanding Actor in a Feature Film in a Crossover Role" for his part in *I Still Know What You Did Last Summer*.

*She's All That* remained popular long after its release. Even two years after its release the movie was chosen as "Best Date Flick" on video by readers of *Teen* magazine. They also gave Prinze the title of "Fave Leading Man" two years in a row.

Prinze did not let his success go to his head. In his typical modesty, he played down the importance of playing the lead. "I think of making movies as a team effort, and sometimes you are the quarterback and sometimes you are the receiver," he said. "Either way, you do your job and you make sure you are great."[4]

His modesty was apparent to those who worked with him. "Freddie's very shy about having any attention drawn to him at all," said director Robert Iscove. "It's pretty refreshing."[5] Harvey Weinstein, chief executive of Miramax, was also impressed with the young actor. "I think as a human being he has great integrity and a wonderful work ethic," he said.[6]

Prinze had reached his dream of stardom in only five years. His success surprised even him. "This is where I wanted to be, but this isn't where I thought I would be," he said. "I saw it taking a bit more time."[7]

The young actor was a rising star. Only time would tell where Prinze's talents would take him.

# 2

# Fatherless

From 1974 to 1976, millions of television viewers tuned in to the popular sitcom *Chico and the Man*. It starred a handsome twenty-year-old comedian named Freddie Prinze. Within a few years, Prinze had grown from a little-known stand-up comic to the star of a hit series. His success was even more unusual because he was half Puerto Rican. At that time, only one other Latino actor had starred in a television series. Desi Arnaz played a leading role in *I Love Lucy*.

As Chico, Prinze was a charming Latino garage mechanic with a twinkle in his eye and an infectious grin. But beneath the laughter was a very depressed young man. He was unable to deal with his rapid rise to fame. Prinze dealt with his depression by turning to drugs and alcohol. He started by smoking marijuana with his friends in high school. When he began performing, he sniffed cocaine because he felt he needed it

Desi Arnaz (front right) was a Cuban American who starred with his wife, Lucille Ball (front left) on the television show *I Love Lucy*. In the back seat are Vivian Vance (left) and William Frawley (right), who played the Mertzes, Lucy and Ricky's neighbors, on the show.

to do his shows. After his shows, he took Valium to help him relax enough to sleep.

On the surface, Prinze seemed to have everything going for him. He had a successful and exciting career. In 1975, he married Katherine Elaine Cochran. In March 1976, *Chico and the Man* was renewed for its third season. Then, in one of the most important events in Prinze's life, his wife gave birth to their son. Freddie James Prinze, Jr., arrived on March 8, 1976.

Prinze, Sr., witnessed the birth of his son. He later wrote in his diary, "He is a miracle baby and I love my family. I am on top of the world no matter what happens. The lord has saved me again."[1]

But Prinze's life was not saved. He sank back into his

**Freddie Prinze, Sr., is shown toasting with his bride, Katherine Cochran, on their wedding day in Las Vegas on October 13, 1975.**

destructive lifestyle of abusing drugs and alcohol. The quaaludes his doctor prescribed to help him relax hurt him the most. Depression is one side effect of the hypnotic drug, and it hit Prinze hard.

Prinze's drug abuse worried Kathy Cochran. She was concerned about the safety of their baby. She sent Freddie, Jr., to Albuquerque to stay with her parents for awhile. Losing his son only made Prinze sink deeper into depression. Cochran brought little Freddie back home. By then, it was apparent that she could not stay married to Prinze. She filed for divorce.

At that point, Prinze's life caved in around him. He had lost his wife and son. He faced charges of driving while under the influence of drugs. He was involved in an expensive lawsuit with his former manager.

Prinze's deep depression, his dependence on drugs, and his fascination with guns proved to be a deadly combination. The morning of January 28, 1977, he shot himself in the head in front of his business manager. He died in a hospital the next day. "I can't take any more. It's all my fault. There is no one to blame but me," read the note he left behind.[2] Freddie Prinze was only twenty-two years old. Ten-month-old Freddie, Jr., had to grow up without a father.

At first, Freddie Prinze's death was ruled a suicide. As a result, his family could not collect on his life insurance policies. Several years later, Prinze's mother, Maria Pruetzel, got the ruling overturned. A jury decided that Prinze's death had been accidental. He had taken so

## A Famous Father

Freddie Prinze, born Frederick Karl Pruetzel, grew up in a working-class area of New York City. As a child, the sensitive, overweight boy was the target of bullies who picked on him and took his lunch money. Freddie learned early that humor could get him out of some unpleasant situations.

Although he was not an outstanding student, Freddie had enough talent to be accepted into the exclusive High School for Performing Arts. He acted in some of their stage productions, but found comedy more to his liking. "I started doing half-hour routines in the boy's room, just winging it. Guys cut class to catch the act. It was, 'What time's Freddie playing the toilet today?'" Prinze, Sr., joked.[3]

When he started performing, Freddie Pruetzel felt he needed a new name. "I cannot be the king of comedy because Bob Hope is already the king, but I will be the prince," he said.[4] Freddie changed the spelling to Prinze to make it more unique.

Prinze learned his craft by studying other comedians and by performing in local comedy clubs. He dropped out of high school a month before graduation to pursue his career. An appearance on Johnny Carson's *Tonight Show* at age nineteen gave the young comedian national recognition. His appearance accelerated his rapid rise to fame.

many quaaludes, a strong sedative, that he did not know what he was doing.

Cochran and Pruetzel felt that two of Prinze's doctors contributed to his death. One was his psychiatrist, a doctor who treats mental and emotional disorders. They blamed him for returning a pistol to Prinze the night he shot himself. They also blamed Prinze's internist, a doctor who deals with diseases of the internal organs. He was responsible for overprescribing quaaludes. In 1981, the two doctors settled with the family for a total of nine hundred fifty thousand dollars.

Cochran wanted Freddie to have a normal upbringing. She knew that staying in Los Angeles would make that job harder. Too many people there knew about his father's tragic death. Before Freddie turned four, he and his mother moved to Albuquerque,

> "My granny is the closest person in the world to me."

New Mexico, to be near Cochran's parents. "I was raised by my mother and my maternal grandparents," Freddie said. "My granny is the closest person in the world to me."[5]

Freddie had no memories of his father. His mother filled him in on the good things about the man he never knew. "My mother told me about how much he loved me and the way his face would light up when he held me," Freddie said later.[6] He also learned that his father's special nickname for him was "Pie." He never knew why his father chose that particular nickname.

Freddie grew up in a loving home, but being an only child with no father was lonely at times. He escaped by burying himself in comic books and cartoons. He made up imaginary friends to play with. None of this seemed unusual to Freddie. It was his way of dealing with his life.

His love of make-believe gave Freddie the scar still visible on his chin. When he was about five years old, he and his cousin Nicky were playing *Star Wars*. Freddie played Luke Skywalker while Nicky played Darth Vader. They broke a metal flagpole in half to make their lightsabers. As Freddie escaped down a slide he fell on the sharp end of the pole and cut his chin. The accident may have scarred his face, but it did nothing to dampen his love of pretending.

Another outlet for Freddie's creativity was the Albuquerque Children's Theater. Sue Ann Gunn, the assistant director at the time, called Freddie "a bright, energetic and willing student."[7] As they worked on plays, Freddie often suggested ideas and Gunn let him try them out. In the play *The Traveling Bandit Show*, Freddie threw himself into his role as Horatio Hateful, the villain in the melodrama. As a teenager, he got involved in a local theater group called the Duo Drama Company.

Freddie's family made sure that he was exposed to a lot of different activities as he grew up. He took lessons in swimming and dancing. He especially enjoyed boxing and martial arts. It did not hurt that his godfather was martial arts expert Bob Wall, who had appeared in some Bruce Lee movies.

Like a lot of young boys, Freddie also tried his hand at Little League baseball. In the beginning, he was far from being the star of the team. "I was a 'pitcher.' But we had a pitching machine, so I was just basically an 'in-infield' shortstop because all I got to do was field bloopers six feet from the plate. I couldn't hit, so that was pretty much my entire job," he recalled.[8]

Freddie may not have set the world on fire in Little League, but he was a big baseball fan. He followed the Dukes, a Triple A affiliate of the Dodgers that played in Albuquerque at that time. He even got a chance to serve as batboy for the team at age ten.

When he was young, Freddie assumed that his family was like everyone else's. Then he realized that all his friends had fathers, something he did not have. "It hurt a lot growing up. As I got older, sometimes I became angry because almost everybody I knew had an old man except me. That wears on you after a while. It becomes like a rock that you have to push up a hill, which eventually rolls you over."[9]

As time went on, Freddie became more curious about his father. His mother freely shared the good things about him. But, talking about his father's dark side was harder. Cochran wanted to protect her son from the unpleasant details. "Nobody could really talk to me about it, because everybody was kind of like scared and they did not know the right words to say," Freddie said. "They didn't want to tell me that my old man did drugs and shot himself."[10]

Freddie learned the truth during an argument with a classmate when he was about thirteen. "A kid said, 'Your dad was a junkie who killed himself and you're going to end up the same way.' I had thought my dad was prescribed pills and died of a drug overdose. I knew there was a gun involved, but not really exactly how."[11]

> *"If only he had known how great a son I could have been, there's no way he'd have done that!"*

"After learning that, I hated my dad for what he'd done," Prinze admitted. "I felt like I didn't get a chance to be his son. If only he had known how great a son I could have been, there's no way he'd have done that!"[12]

During a trip to California, family friend Ron DiBlasio told Freddie both the good and the bad things about his father. "We stopped in front of Marilyn Monroe's house, and he said, 'You know she died too, before she should have. She was the biggest star in the world, but she didn't know how to deal with her pain.'"[13]

Freddie Prinze, Jr., had some rough times as a child, but he did not know how bad it could get until he reached high school.

# 3

# The Outsider

Freddie Prinze, Jr., was not a big believer in astrology. Still, he was once curious enough to look up his birthday in an astrology book. March 8 was called "The Day of Nonconformity." As he remembered, the description read: "You don't believe in conforming to the majority. You pull for the underdog. You always go against the grain—not to cause problems, but because you have to follow your own tune."[1]

It was "following his own tune" that made Freddie's adolescent years difficult. He began his freshman year at El Dorado High School in 1990. It began the period of his life when he felt most like an outsider.

"Being a teenager is the roughest [time of your life] and that's when your emotions are going 90 mph," Freddie said. "I'd get angry or sad or I isolated myself a little and then I looked for help. I didn't know how to deal with all these emotions."[2]

Freddie tried team sports as a way to fit in, but it did not work. He was too slow and too inept at making shots to be on the basketball team. Trying out for the football team was not much better. The quarterback threw him a pass that nearly knocked him over. The coach suggested that he not come back the next day.

Playing on the soccer team did little to help Freddie's image. "I was so bad that I scored a goal on my own team in [a soccer game]. [I kicked the ball into] my own goal. . . . we lost the game [1–0]."[3] His own team may have been mad, but his opponents loved him. They told him that he was the best player on their team.

> "I was so bad that I scored a goal on my own team."

Although he never won a high school letter for sports, Freddie was not a total klutz. Individual sports proved to be a better fit. He excelled in boxing, skiing, and martial arts.

Freddie had a few close friends, but that did not keep him from being shunned by most of his classmates. He coped with the painful parts of his life by escaping into a fantasy world. Lunch hours were often spent acting out scenes from movies he had seen. *Ferris Bueller's Day Off* was one of his favorites. At other times, Freddie created his own stories to act out. He made up a character for the X-Men, the team of superheroes he read about in comic books. Freddie named his character

One of Freddie Prinze, Jr.'s favorite movies growing up was *Ferris Bueller's Day Off*. Above, from right, Matthew Broderick, Mia Sara, and Alan Ruck act in a scene from the film.

"Prism" after the glass that splits light into the colors of the rainbow.

Much like Freddie, Prism was a boy who did not fit in. He was an outcast because he could not control his powers. Instead of being focused, his powers shot out in all directions. Help came from Professor X, the kindly instructor for the X-Men. He taught Prism how to focus his powers.

While Freddie's playacting helped him escape, it did nothing to gain him acceptance with his classmates.

They thought he was weird. They could not understand someone who spent his lunch hours on the soccer field dodging the magnetic blasts from imaginary enemies. They thought it was odd for someone to sneak off to the empty wrestling room to reenact fantasies. Freddie knew that he was weird, but it did not stop him. "That's what I loved to do," he later said.[4]

Although Freddie looked for ways to escape his problems, he never resorted to using drugs. They had ruined his life enough already by cheating him out of having a dad. Through his death, his father had shown him how deeply someone's actions could hurt the people he loved the most. It was the only lesson his father had been able to teach him.

*He learned to speak Spanish and became familiar with his Puerto Rican heritage.*

His father was not around to support Freddie at this difficult time. However, Freddie's mother made sure that he was never cut off from his father's family. When his grandmother, Maria Pruetzel, moved back to Puerto Rico, Freddie often visited her during his vacations. There, he learned to speak Spanish and became familiar with his Puerto Rican heritage. It balanced out the Italian culture of his mother's family.

When Freddie and his mother moved, he changed

**Freddie Prinze, Jr., sometimes visited relatives in Puerto Rico. Pictured is the island's capital city, San Juan.**

## Puerto Rico

While growing up, Freddie often spent vacations with his grandmother in Puerto Rico. Each year, millions of tourists visit the tropical island 1,000 miles southeast of Miami, Florida. They enjoy the warm temperatures, sandy beaches, and clear water. Others like the mountains that stretch across the "Island of Enchantment."

Puerto Rico is a commonwealth of the United States. Its people are U.S. citizens. They can travel to the United States to live, work, or visit whenever they want. Puerto Ricans have their own government to handle local issues. In other areas, they follow the laws of the United States.

to Sandia High School for his sophomore year. It may have been a different school, but life was much the same. His new classmates also had trouble understanding Freddie's bizarre behavior. He dated, but his relationships were short-lived. "I had like 80 girlfriends and they all dumped me in like 3 days," he joked.[5]

Another move meant another change in schools. Freddie transferred to La Cueva High School at the beginning of his junior year. Again the other students quickly pegged him as an oddball. One teacher was so concerned that she suggested that Freddie's mother take him for counseling.

"All you do is live on other people's lives, and you're never going to exist in the real world," the counselor told him.[6] Freddie listened to what she said, then went back to living his own life.

Although Freddie was considered odd by many of his classmates, he did have a small circle of close friends. Some of those friendships are still intact today. In the winter, he and his friends enjoyed skiing together in the mountains around Albuquerque. Freddie became quite good. During his senior year, he worked three days a week for the ski patrol in Santa Fe. His job brought in some much needed money, but it did nothing to improve his grades. Freddie had to skip school one day a week to squeeze in his third day of work. "I had 48 absences in the winter semester of my senior year and graduated with a D average," Freddie admitted.[7]

At first, Freddie's mother did not realize how much he was skipping school. She was upset when he almost got expelled over his absences. Her pleas to the principal allowed Freddie to avoid expulsion.

In one respect, Freddie and his father were alike when it came to school. They worked hard in the subjects that inter-

*"I had 48 absences in the winter semester of my senior year."*

ested them, but slid through the others. One subject that Freddie enjoyed was literature. During his senior year, his literature class studied the Greek tragedy *Oedipus Rex*. His teacher, Patsy Boeglin, asked Freddie to read part of it aloud. "I think everybody could see his passion," Boeglin said.[8]

As high school graduation neared, Freddie's family faced some hard times. His beloved maternal grandfather passed away. Then his mother faced financial setbacks that forced her to sell their home.

> "Once my heart gets set on something, that's it."

Prinze graduated from La Cueva High School in the spring of 1994. His future stretched out before him, but he was not sure what to do with it. Cochran tried to steer her son toward becoming an environmental engineer. Prinze at one time had thought about becoming a psychologist. But those careers required a college degree, which was not an option at that time. He had neither the grades nor the money to go to college.

Prinze needed to find a career that did not require a college degree. He did not want to get trapped in a low-paying job, such as bagging groceries at Price Club. He did not have a lot of skills, other than acting out his fantasies. Trying his hand at performing seemed like his best option.

Cochran was not enthusiastic about her son's career choice. She had watched fame destroy her husband. She did not want to see the same thing happen to her son. "She wasn't nuts about the idea for obvious reasons," Prinze said. "But my mother has always known that once my heart gets set on something, that's it. Whether I'm wrong or right, she accepts it. And either way, I'm gonna do it."[9]

In the fall of 1994, Prinze loaded all his belongings into a beat-up jeep and headed west to Los Angeles. "I had no money. I had no job. And I barely had a high school education because I hardly ever went," he said.[10] But Prinze had a dream and the fierce determination to make it come true.

# 4

# Risky Move

At eighteen years of age, Freddie Prinze, Jr., was on his way to an unknown future. "It was really scary," Prinze said about his drive to Los Angeles. "I was sure that being the son of a dead celebrity was not going to open any doors for me. But I just didn't know what else to do with my life."[1]

When he reached Los Angeles, Prinze moved in with one of his mother's close friends. Her family owned the Valley Ranch Barbecue Restaurant. They gave Prinze a job until he got on his feet. The pay was meager, but it helped pay for acting classes and other necessities.

Prinze began his life in Los Angeles with a severe case of homesickness. He missed having his friends and his mother and grandmother around. He threw himself into his acting classes to take his mind off his loneliness. Unlike some of his high school subjects, which he found boring, he became completely absorbed with acting.

He had no time for girlfriends, buddies, or any kind of social life. "All I did was just eat, drink and sleep acting," Prinze remembered.[2]

At his mother's suggestion, Prinze visited Jay Leno, host of the *Tonight Show*. Leno and Freddie Prinze, Sr., had been friends when both were starting out as stand-up comedians. Leno even taught Prinze, Sr., how to drive, but that may not be a compliment. Prinze, Sr., had a reputation as an awful driver.

As a newcomer, Prinze, Jr., did not understand how things worked in Hollywood. He strolled into the NBC studios and told the guard that he wanted to see Jay Leno. The guard turned down the teenager's request. Prinze tried to explain that his father had been a friend of Leno's. The guard held firm. Finally Prinze said,

Freddie Prinze, Jr., moved to California to try to make a name for himself in Hollywood.

"Please would you just call him? My name's Freddie Prinze, Jr. My dad was Freddie Prinze, he was friends with Jay."[3] The guard made the call and a few minutes later a lady arrived to escort Prinze to Leno's office.

Leno shared his memories of Prinze's father. He also gave Prinze some tapes of *Chico and the Man* so he could see his father in action.

Prinze picked up bits of advice from various people in the business. Some suggested that he become a stand-up comedian like his father. "Apparently you have to be very funny to do that and I'm a lot better if somebody writes it down first," Prinze later told David Letterman.[4]

The people Prinze talked to were nice to him, but their connections did not translate into jobs. It reconfirmed what Prinze already knew. His name alone was not going to open any doors. His success would depend entirely on him.

"I'd made a choice," Prinze said. "I'd gone to L.A. because I had to find a challenge. I believed that, as long as I didn't quit on myself, I couldn't fail. Nothing could stop me but me."[5]

The next step for Prinze was to find an agent to help guide his career. An agent would be able to get him into more and better auditions. Some that he talked to had suggestions for things Prinze should do to become more successful. One suggestion was that he change his name to avoid being compared to his father. That was something Prinze refused to do. "My name was something my father wanted to give me and he wasn't able to give me a lot," Prinze explained.[6]

Shortly after Prinze left home, his mother moved to Las Vegas where she worked as a real estate agent. Her main reason for going to Albuquerque fourteen years earlier had been to give her son a normal life. Now, with Prinze on his own, she could move on with her life.

Prinze also moved again. After living with family friends for a few months, he moved into his own apartment. His living quarters were small, and not in the best part of town. Still, he could call it a place of his own. The biggest problem was trying to scrape together six hundred dollars every month to pay the rent. Sometimes he was so broke that he hid in his apartment. He hoped the landlord would not realize that he was home. That was hard to do since he lived on the second floor. He had to pass the landlord's apartment every time he left.

"The landlord would pound on my door screaming 'I know you're in there!' I would just sit on the floor with the lights out and pray my manager would call [with a job]. But I couldn't answer the phone because the landlord would know that I was there."[7]

In the beginning, Prinze was turned down for every role he auditioned for. For several months, he had faced nothing but rejection. He began having bouts of depression. "I had started doubting and questioning what I was doing with my life," he said. "My greatest fear was ending up like my father."[8]

One day, Prinze hit bottom. His doubts and frustrations completely overwhelmed him. "I was sitting in my car. I suddenly started crying—big, heavy, aching sobs. It was terrifying. I felt this huge weight that was just crushing me," he said.[9]

Then he looked up and saw his eyes in the rearview mirror. "Suddenly everything was cool. I knew I wasn't going to end up like my dad. It was as if God said, 'You don't need to worry anymore' and from then on everything went into place."[10]

While waiting for his career to take off, Prinze came up with a backup plan. He had always loved to cook, so he enrolled in culinary school in Pasadena. He continued taking acting classes, studying, and going to auditions. Finally, he had a glimmer of success. He earned a small guest role in the television sitcom *Family Matters*. His character was a punk who brought a gun to school. The role was small—only four lines. Still, it was a real acting job with a real paycheck. "That was my big break and I thought it was huge," he said.[11]

Prinze wanted to share the moment with the father he had never known. He made his first trip to the Forest Lawn cemetery to visit his father's grave. "I put my hand on his plaque and I said, 'Thank you. I hope you're watching now. I hope to make you proud.'"[12]

Although Prinze's first role on *Family Matters* excited him, he chose not to watch the episode that gave him his start. The role of playing a delinquent with a gun was too common among the roles offered to Hispanic actors at that time. "People have to understand: Growing up as a Puerto Rican in this business is very hard unless you want [your character] to sell drugs, or be a pimp, or carry a gun. And I refused to do that."[13]

He remembered a quote by Louis Gossett, Jr., referring to his Oscar-winning role in the movie *An Officer and a Gentleman*. "He told his agent he would not

## In the Minority

In 2004, Latinos made up over 14 percent of the population of the United States. Yet a Children Now report from the same year found that only 6 percent of prime-time television characters were Latino. Most of them were shown in low-paying, unskilled jobs. Many were depicted as criminals. Whites were three times as likely to be seen in professional roles, such as doctors or lawyers.[14]

Many groups have been working to improve the employment picture for Latinos. Their efforts are paying off both onscreen and behind the scenes. In 2002, *The George Lopez Show* became the first series since *I Love Lucy* to depict a Latino family. In 2005, about ten new series on the major networks featured Latino actors in important roles. Popular shows such as *Desperate Housewives* and ABC's *Lost* had diverse casts. By the end of 2006, ABC had Latinos regularly appearing in all their top-rated programs. In 2007, America Ferrera won the Emmy Award as "Best Actress in a Comedy" for her show, *Ugly Betty*.

**Prinze, Jr., played opposite Jessica Alba as a teen father-to-be in the made-for-TV movie *Too Soon for Jeff*.**

read for an African American role—he only wanted to read for the roles the white actors were going up for. I took the same strategy," said Prinze.[15]

Movies and television influence the way people see the world. They affect the way Latinos and other minorities are viewed and even how they see themselves. Although gains are being made, more work is needed to include all minority groups.

Although it may not have been the ideal role, appearing on *Family Matters* allowed Prinze to get his foot in the door. It was not long before another television role pushed that door open a little wider.

Soon after his *Family Matters* appearance, Prinze won the lead in an ABC Afterschool Special, *Too Soon for Jeff*. He played the role of Jeff, a high school senior with a college scholarship and a promising future. Jeff's life was turned upside down when his girlfriend announced that she was pregnant. He had to choose between accepting his scholarship and facing the responsibilities of fatherhood.

Prinze told a small lie to get the lead role. His agent had sent him to audition for one of the supporting characters. When Prinze arrived, he told them that he was there to read for the role of Jeff. He had not even looked at his lines before he got to the audition. Even reading it cold, Prinze was good enough to capture the part. A few weeks later, the director discovered what Prinze had done. However, he saw no reason to boot Prinze out of the starring role.

With two appearances behind him, Prinze's career began to move forward. Not long after completing *Too Soon for Jeff*, he received his first movie role. It was in an independent film titled *To Gillian on Her 37th Birthday*. Prinze's role was small, but it gave him the opportunity to work with some big names—Michelle Pfeiffer, Peter Gallagher, Kathy Baker, and Claire Danes. The movie had a budget of only $10 million, which was very low by Hollywood standards. But the stars were impressed enough with the script to work for less money than usual.

*To Gillian on Her 37th Birthday* is about a widower (Gallagher) who cannot get over the death of his wife in a boating accident two years earlier. He spends much of his time frolicking on the beach with his wife's ghost. This leaves him little time to cope with his teenage daughter Rachel (Danes), who is still grieving over the loss of her mother. She desperately needs her father's attention. To fill the void, Rachel turns to Joey (Prinze). Although he looks tough on the outside, Joey has a sensitive nature. He helps bring the father and daughter together again.

For Prinze, working on *To Gillian on Her 37th Birthday* was like going to acting class every day. He constantly learned from the high-caliber actors that surrounded him. He watched everything they did and listened to their advice. He enjoyed all the people he worked with, but Danes really got his heart pumping.

Prinze admits to having a crush on Danes. "She would

**Claire Danes was the recipient of Freddie Prinze Jr.'s first on-screen kiss. Above is a scene from the movie they acted in together, *To Gillian on Her 37th Birthday*.**

come up to me, just to say hello, and my stomach would be like in 8,000 knots. I'd practically have to run off to the dressing room to throw up."[16]

His crush on Danes made him even more anxious about his first on-screen kiss. While he was waiting to be called for the scene, he was so nervous he was shaking. "I got down on my hands and knees and I was like, 'Dear God, I'm not trying to be cool or smooth or anything just PLEASE don't let me throw up on this girl.'"[17]

Everyone on the set knew about his crush. Peter

Gallagher, who played Danes' father, was supposed to break up the kiss. Gallagher was slow in making his entrance, leaving Prinze and Danes lip-locked longer than planned.

*To Gillian on Her 37th Birthday* was released in 1996. After that, Prinze's life began to come together. He had finished his first movie role and had more prospects lined up. His social life had improved to the point that he began dating. However, he had never been part of a serious relationship. Pretty soon, there would be someone to change that.

# Growth Spurt

In January 1996, Prinze appeared on the Golden Globe Awards. He was named "Mr. Golden Globe," an honorary title given to the child of a famous actor. His only duty was to help hand out the awards. Still, it gave Prinze some exposure.

Kimberly McCullough, a seventeen-year-old soap opera star, watched the Golden Globes from home that night. She and Prinze had been in the same acting class at one time, but they had never spoken. That is not to say that McCullough had not noticed the handsome young actor. She told a mutual friend that she thought Prinze was cute. The friend delivered the bad news that he already had a girlfriend.

At that time, McCullough was more famous than Prinze. The actress had been working since doing a diaper commercial at age two. In 1985, at age seven, she became a regular on the soap opera *General Hospital*.

She played the part of Robin Soltini Scorpio. At eleven, McCullough won her first Daytime Emmy for "Outstanding Juvenile Female in a Drama Series." In 1995, the storyline had Robin involved with Stone Cates in her first real romance. Tragedy struck when Stone was diagnosed with AIDS. Robin discovered that she was HIV positive. The controversial storyline earned McCullough another Daytime Emmy for "Outstanding Younger Leading Actress in a Drama Series."

Fortunately for McCullough, her real-life romance had less drama. The same night that she saw Prinze on the Golden Globes, her friend called to say that Prinze had broken up with his girlfriend. She offered to give Prinze McCullough's phone number.

> *"I was thinking 'How did he know I loved to ice skate? Who is this guy?'"*
> —Kimberly McCullough, actress and Prinze's first serious girlfriend

The night of their first date, Prinze arrived at McCullough's home with a bouquet of flowers. He offered to take her anywhere she wanted to go. They chose a Japanese restaurant. Then Prinze suggested that they go ice skating after dinner.

"I was thinking 'How did he know I loved to ice skate? Who is this guy?'" McCullough remembered. "He's the most honest, gentle, sweetest man you'll ever meet. You like him instantly. He has a smile that lights up his face."[1]

Taking McCullough skating fit perfectly with Prinze's theory about first dates. He thought movies were a bad idea. "You're not learning anything about the person," he explained. "You're not even looking at her. And you'll kiss a lot more if you don't go to the movies."[2]

Prinze thought physical activities, such as miniature golf, bowling, and ice skating, were more romantic. "You gotta do something cheesy so you can laugh together," he said. "And it should be something that lets you maintain physical contact, like ice skating where you might slip and she'll have to help you up and you have a nice moment."[3]

Having a date that liked to eat was a plus for Prinze. "You don't have to be thin as a board to be hot," he said. "I'll say, 'You look hungry. I'm not kissing you till you're full because I'm afraid you're going to bite my lip.'"[4]

His dating philosophy proved to be successful. Prinze's first date with McCullough soon led to his first serious relationship. Life was good. He was in love, and his career was on the move.

Prinze's next role was a part in the television drama *Detention: The Siege at Johnson High*, which aired in 1997. Appearing in *Detention* gave Prinze the chance to work with two more established actors. Rick Schroder (*NYPD Blue*) played the part of Jason, a psychotic killer. Henry Winkler (*Happy Days*) was Skip Fine, a small-time cop

Actor Freddie Prinze, Jr., poses with actress Kimberly McCullough on August 24, 1998, at the premiere of *54* in Hollywood. The two were dating at the time.

pushed into the role of negotiator. The drama was based on a real-life shooting and hostage situation that took place in Olivehurst, California, in 1992.

In the movie, Jason goes on a killing rampage at his former high school. He guns down a popular teacher and takes eighty terrified students hostage. One of those hostages is a troubled student named Aaron Sullivan (Prinze). Aaron becomes the middleman between the gunman and Skip Fine. Although several students are killed, Aaron helps end the situation before more lives are lost.

Prinze went from a high school tragedy to a quirky dark comedy. He was part of the cast for the independent film *The House of Yes*. The story involves the dysfunctional Pascal family. Marty Pascal (Josh Hamilton) brings his new fiancée Lesly (Tori Spelling) home for Thanksgiving dinner to meet his unusual family. Marty's twin sister, Jackie (Parker Posey), is obsessed with Jacqueline Kennedy Onassis, widow of assassinated president John F. Kennedy. She dresses like Onassis and enjoys dramatizing JFK's murder using spaghetti sauce for blood. Jackie had carried on an incestuous relationship with her twin brother, Marty. Prinze is the younger brother, Anthony, who is not much better. "He was like a Norman Bates [from the movie *Psycho*] before his mom bought the motel," Prinze said. "You knew he was going to snap and something was just a little bit off."[5]

Filming *The House of Yes* had some challenging

## Indies

Prinze's first films, such as *To Gillian on Her 37th Birthday* and *The House of Yes*, were "indies." These are independent films made outside the major movie studios. Not being under the thumb of a studio gives indies more creative freedom. They can tackle subjects that mainstream studios would be afraid to try. Many well-known actors accept roles in indies. However, the independent films also give exposure to directors and actors who are not yet famous enough to interest large studios.

Major studios want movies that generate millions of dollars in profits. They prefer high-action blockbusters, big name stars, and spectacular special effects. These films are very expensive to produce. Indies are usually filmed on a limited budget. In 1997, *The House of Yes* had a budget of about $1.5 million. The same year, *Batman & Robin's* budget was $125 million. To cut expenses, producers pay actors in indies less and filming is streamlined.

Some films are true independents, produced by individuals or small production companies with little outside help. However, many major movie studios now have their own companies, such as Miramax, to distribute indies. This helps more independent films get into theaters, but once again may put them under the control of the parent companies.

From left to right, Tori Spelling, Parker Posey, Josh Hamilton, and Freddie Prinze, Jr., act out a scene in *The House of Yes*.

moments for Prinze. He was still inexperienced in the area of on-screen romancing. The first take of his love scene with Tori Spelling was anything but smooth. "I kissed her eye. I kissed her ear," he remembered. "I'm not smooth with women at all."[6] By then, Prinze realized the humor in his situation. After a good laugh, he settled down enough to finish the scene.

Working on *The House of Yes* was a turning point in Prinze's career. "I think it was the film that really changed me and brought me a little bit of respect," he said. He was especially impressed with the passion shown by director Mark Waters and the acting talents of Posey. "Because of their passion and love of their craft, I fell in love with acting."[7]

*The House of Yes* was well received at the Sundance Film Festival in January 1997. Miramax agreed to distribute the movie. It was released in a limited number of theaters across the country in October of that year.

Prinze knew, as an independent film, the movie would attract little notice. It was shown mostly in smaller art theaters. Its "R" rating kept many of his fans from seeing it. Still, working on it had made an impact on Prinze's life and his career.

Prinze was twenty-one when he finished filming *The House of Yes*. He was not wealthy, but at least he no longer had to hide from his landlord. He could finally afford to move out of his tiny apartment. He moved into a house in North Hollywood with two of his friends.

As Prinze's acting career grew, so did his love for McCullough. He enjoyed being around her and loved being in a stable relationship. He missed her whenever he had to go on location for filming. But McCullough was young. She had been working as an actress nearly all her life. Now that she was eighteen, it was time to think about her future. She did not want to be in soap operas forever. After much thought, she decided to go to film school at New York University. This meant that she and Prinze would be living on opposite sides of the continent. Prinze knew he would miss her, but he loved her too much to stand in the way of her goals. In August 1996, McCullough left for New York City. She and Prinze vowed to do everything they could to keep their long-distance relationship alive.

With McCullough gone, Prinze filled the void with acting. He became more recognized in the movie industry, but that did not guarantee success in winning parts. He auditioned for a role in a teenage horror film called *Scary Movie*. The title of the film written by Kevin Williamson was later changed to *Scream*. Prinze had always been a fan of horror movies, and felt that he was right for the part of Stuart. His audition seemed to have gone well and he expected to get the part. Much to his disappointment, Matthew Lillard was chosen for the role. Still, the audition had not been a waste of time. Kevin Williamson had plans that would play an important part in Prinze's future.

# Sizzling Summers

Kevin Williamson likes horror. His screenplay for the movie *Scream* had been a success. Now he was ready to try again. He loosely based his next project on a young adult novel by Lois Duncan. He had not forgotten Prinze's audition for *Scream*. He sent Prinze a copy of the script for his new horror film, *I Know What You Did Last Summer*.

Prinze was startled when he first received the script. The title immediately sparked a memory. He read Duncan's book when he was in the fourth grade. "After I read the book, I was terrified for a month and didn't want to sleep or anything and then, suddenly, ten years later I opened a script and the title, in big, huge, frightening letters, said *I Know What You Did Last Summer*. I had the biggest flashback."[1]

Prinze felt that he was right for the part of Ray, a young man who did not fit in well with the rest of the crowd. Auditioning for the role was frustrating. The director and casting director made him read for the part so many times that Prinze almost gave up. Two weeks after his last audition, the studio called and asked him to come in for still another meeting. By that time, Prinze was fed up.

"I went in and said, 'What's going on? Do you want me to make this movie or not, 'cause if not, I'll go make another one,'" Prinze said.[2] They explained that they were still interested. They had just wanted to meet with him one more time. Four hours later, he got the part.

Joining Prinze on the set were three other popular teen actors. Jennifer Love Hewitt played the part of Ray's girl-friend, Julie. Sarah Michelle Gellar played Helen, a smart but insecure beauty queen. Ryan Phillippe was cast as Helen's boyfriend, Barry, a popular high school football player.

> "What's going on? Do you want me to make this movie or not?"

The plot of the teen slasher movie involves a deadly accident and a poor decision. Driving home from a night of partying, the four friends hit a man on Reaper's Curve. To their horror, they discover that the victim is dead. Julie wants to do the right thing and call the police. Her friends talk her out of it. They do not want to jeopardize their future plans. Ray, who had been

## Appalled Author

*I Know What You Did Last Summer* was a hit, but not with the author who wrote the book. "I was appalled when my book . . . was made into a slasher film," Lois Duncan said.[3]

When authors sell the movie rights to their books, they usually have no control over the finished product. Kevin Williamson used Duncan's book as the basis for his screenplay. He needed to add more violence and gruesome scenes to change the story from a psychological thriller into a horror movie.

In Duncan's book, only one person dies. Four teenagers accidentally kill a boy on a bicycle. One of the teenagers is shot, but recovers. Duncan said that her story is "about the importance of resisting peer pressure and of taking responsibility for your actions."[4]

Duncan had good reason to be against violence. Eight years before the movie came out, her eighteen-year-old daughter, Kaitlyn, was murdered. "As the mother of a murdered child, I don't find violent death something to squeal and giggle about," she said.[5]

driving the car, convinces Julie to go along with the crowd. They dump the body in the ocean and pretend that the accident never happened.

When Julie returns home from college the next summer, she receives an unsigned note saying only "I know what you did last summer." The four friends spend the summer being stalked by a crazed serial killer wearing a black fisherman's slicker and carrying a deadly ice hook.

Ray is the outsider of the group. While the other three come from money, he has to work for everything he gets. He loves Julie and tries hard to fit in with her friends. Prinze had no trouble understanding how Ray felt. "Ray is a loner," he said. "He's experienced a lot more real life than the other characters . . . I also feel like I grew up differently from other kids."[6]

Prinze was unlike his character in one respect. Ray gives in to peer pressure. Going against his beliefs nearly kills him. As a teenager, Prinze remained true to himself. He went his own way, even when it kept him from being accepted by his peers.

> *Prinze was happy when the filming ended.*

*I Know What You Did Last Summer* was filmed in the isolated area of Southport, North Carolina. Much of the filming took place at night. A typical workday for the actors began about 10:00 P.M. At midnight they would assemble in a large tent for lunch. Then it was back to work until quitting time, about 7:30 A.M.

Prinze was happy when the filming ended. He looked forward to spending time with McCullough who was coming home for the summer. She moved in with Prinze and his two roommates. Fortunately, the roommates liked her and did not mind the addition to their household.

At the end of the summer, McCullough made the difficult decision to go back to film school in New York. "I actually went back to start my second year, but three days before school started, I freaked out and said, 'No, I don't want to buy my books, I don't want to go to school and I don't want to register,' so I came home right after that."[7]

McCullough returned to her role as Robin Scorpio in *General Hospital*. She did not sign a long-term contract with the show. At that point, she was still trying to figure out what she wanted to do with her life. At least for now, she and Prinze could be together.

*I Know What You Did Last Summer* opened in theaters in October 1997. It was a hit, holding the number one spot for three weeks straight. The movie, which cost an estimated $17 million to make, earned back nearly $16 million its first weekend. It went on to gross over $125 million worldwide, making it one of the top-grossing horror films of all time.[8]

The movie's success brought Prinze a lot of recognition and hordes of fans. Most of his encounters were harmless. He laughed about one girl who ran off with his sandwich. He was eating lunch at an airport when a

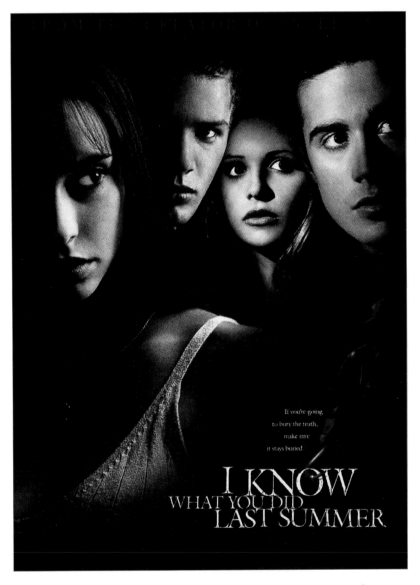

An official movie poster from *I Know What You Did Last Summer* shows, from left to right, Jennifer Love Hewitt, Ryan Phillippe, Sarah Michelle Gellar, and Freddie Prinze, Jr.

fan stopped at his table and asked for his autograph. "I was signing her autograph when her friend runs by and steals my sandwich, I took one bite. She was like 'Oh my God, you're you!' and she grabbed my sandwich and ran away."[9]

In spite of the admiration from fans, Prinze managed to stay grounded. His relationship with McCullough remained solid. The two were not quite ready for marriage, but they took another big step. They decided to buy a house together. Before Prinze had a chance to do much house hunting, he had to leave for Europe. His next movie was being filmed in Luxembourg. Although he was not excited about the location, the role he was playing seemed like a dream come true.

> "I was signing her autograph when her friend . . . steals my sandwich."

Prinze loved playing computer games. One of his favorites was a science-fiction action game called *Wing Commander*. The game's creator, Chris Roberts, turned it into a movie. Prinze won the chance to play the rebellious rookie space pilot, Christopher Blair.

Not everyone was pleased to have Prinze cast in the lead role. Some thought the part should have gone to Mark Hamill, who was the voice actor for Blair in the game. Prinze reminded everyone that the character was twenty-two years old. Hamill was much older than that.

Roberts defended his choice. "Obviously, Freddie's a good actor, but there was a nice cross of vulnerability, likeability and a slightly cocky edge. Plus, he's not terribly bad-looking! He brings a nice empathy to the role. I think he's one of the more talented up-and-coming actors out there."[10]

The sets for *Wing Commander* were built inside huge warehouses at a former munitions factory. For Prinze, reporting for work was like going to an amusement park. The soundstage was filled with full-sized models of fighter jets and flight decks. There were also a number of space-age weapons to play with. It was like every kid's dream of being inside a video game.

*Wing Commander* is about a war being raged in space in the year 2564. Blair is a rookie space pilot trying to save the universe from an alien race. Also on the team is a maverick pilot named Maniac (Matthew Lillard) and their attractive superior officer, Deveraux (Saffron Burrows). Together they fight against the alien attack.

Although Prinze was excited about his role in *Wing Commander*, the results disappointed him. Too many changes were made after he signed on to do the project. Prinze also criticized some of the special effects of the film. "The animatronic creatures looked like Garfield," he said.[11] The movie made a poor showing at the box office when it was released.

While Prinze was away filming *Wing Commander*, McCullough searched for a house for the couple. She bought one in Tuluca Lake, although Prinze had not seen it. Still, Prinze was pleased with her choice. He moved in when filming wrapped up in March 1998. As with his other homes, Prinze hung two meaningful accessories on his wall. One was a photograph of his father doing his stand-up comedy act in a nightclub. The other was a framed copy of his father's comedy album, *Looking Good*.

Prinze did not get to enjoy his new home for long. Soon after he returned from Luxembourg, he had to

The film's makeup artist had to apply some cuts and bruises to Freddie Prinze, Jr., during the filming of *I Still Know What You Did Last Summer.*

fulfill his contract to film *I Still Know What You Did Last Summer*. The sequel to the popular horror film was hastily put together to take advantage of the original movie's success. Prinze was not happy about having to be in the sequel, but he had no choice. He was under contract to do it. At least his part had been shortened to give him time to finish filming *Wing Commander*.

Jennifer Love Hewitt returned for the sequel, but many of the people from the original film were not there. The characters played by Sarah Michelle Gellar and Ryan Phillippe had been killed off in the first movie. Joining Prinze and Hewitt in the sequel were pop-singer Brandy, Mekhi Phifer, and Matthew Settle. Another disappointment was losing writer Kevin Williamson and director Jim Gillespie, who had done such a good job with the first movie.

The sequel takes place two years after the tragic accident. Julie has gone back to college and is still plagued by nightmares. When her best friend, Karla (Brandy), wins a trip to the Bahamas, Julie agrees to go along. She invites Ray (Prinze) to go with her, but he turns her down. Will, who Julie describes as "just a friend," takes his place.

As soon as Julie leaves, Ray discovers that the murderous stalker is also going to the island. Ray takes a boat and heads out to warn Julie. Meanwhile, a hurricane leaves the four vacationers stranded with no phones and no way to get off the island. They pass the time in a karaoke bar. As Julie sings, a frightening message appears on her monitor instead of the song lyrics. It says, "*I Still Know What You Did Last Summer*." Again, the hook-wielding killer terrorizes Julie and her friends. As with the original film, a string of mutilated bodies are left behind.

> **Prinze won the Blockbuster Entertainment Award for "Best Supporting Actor—Horror."**

For Prinze, being on location in Mexico meant that, again, he was away from McCullough. Most of the filming for *I Still Know What You Did Last Summer* took place at the El Tucan Martina Resort. It had been deserted since 1992 when an earthquake damaged the resort. It was not a comfortable shoot for the actors. The area was hot, muggy, and covered with bugs.

*I Still Know What You Did Last Summer* opened on November 15, 1998. In spite of its bad reviews, the pre-release hype was enough to fill the theaters. The movie opened at number two at the box office, pulling in $16.5 million its first weekend. It stayed in the top ten for several weeks.[12] Prinze won the Blockbuster Entertainment Award for "Best Supporting Actor— Horror."

Prinze's two horror movies brought him national attention. His list of credits grew, but he still waited for the big break that would push him into stardom. He did not have to wait much longer.

# Hits and Misses

While Prinze filmed *I Still Know What You Did Last Summer*, his agent sent him a script. He liked the story immediately and knew it was something he wanted to do. "I read every new comedy script coming out and this was the first one that treated the teenage audience with respect and dignity and didn't speak down to them at all and I wanted to be a part of it."[1]

The name of the movie with the high school setting was *She's All That*. Filming began only three days after he finished shooting *I Still Know What You Did Last Summer*. Once again, filming spoiled his plans to spend some uninterrupted time with McCullough, but that was part of being an actor.

Playing Zach gave Prinze the chance to experience a much different type of high school life than his own. Zach was popular, athletic, and the president of his class. That was the complete opposite of Prinze's high school days of being shunned by the popular crowd. He could relate more to the character of Laney. Like Laney, Prinze followed his own path despite what his classmates thought of him.

Besides liking the script, Prinze looked forward to working with two of his friends. He and Matthew Lillard had become buddies while filming *Wing Commander*. He had also worked with his costar, Rachael Leigh Cook, in *The House of Yes*.

> ## "Freddie is a doll!"
> —Rachael Leigh Cook, actress in **She's All That**

"Freddie is a doll!" Cook said. "He's one of the nicest guys I know, or probably ever will. He's great to work with, and has a wonderful sense of humor."[2]

Although Prinze was serious about his work, his mischievous side often showed up on the set. He frequently targeted Cook. "He was always making faces when I was trying to do a serious scene," said Cook. "He's there with his finger in his nose trying to make me laugh."[3]

Prinze formed another lasting friendship on the set. He and Dulé Hill discovered that they shared an interest in tap dancing. Prinze had taken dance lessons as a child, but never kept up with it. Hill, on the other hand, had been tap dancing and acting professionally since childhood. He rekindled Prinze's interest in dance and even agreed to teach him. "It is my second passion. I love making music with my feet," Prinze admitted.[4]

Each film that Prinze made gave him a chance to learn new things. Some of the lessons were dramatic. Others were lighthearted. In *She's All That* he learned the quickest way to get muscles. Prinze's lean build was fine for most scenes, but some thought he needed a little improvement to look like a hunk on the beach. A makeup artist worked her magic to make him look more buff. "This lady shaded me, and I looked up and yo! I had a chest!" Prinze said. "They make it look like you have muscles. And it looked real!"[5]

Prinze was proud of *She's All That* and was pleased that teens selected him for several awards. He was a

**Dulé Hill (center) and Freddie Prinze, Jr., act out a scene from *She's All That* with Paul Walker. Hill and Prinze, Jr., both shared an off-screen love of tap dancing.**

good choice for the admiration of teens, and not just because of his talent or good looks. The way he lived his life made him a good role model. "I realize now it's a responsibility that comes with my job. I'm very proud of that and always try to reflect it in my behavior," Prinze said.[6]

Prinze knew all too well how one person's behavior could affect the lives of loved ones. He and his family all suffered from the unwise choices made by his father. "That's why you don't see me out partying and taking drugs and cheating on the woman I love. It's important to me that people see the other side of it," Prinze said. "I've done everything in my current power to make that happen."[7]

> "You don't see me out partying and taking drugs and cheating on the woman I love."

Not all of the attention that Prinze received was good. He became uncomfortable when his home address became known. Some of the fans pestering him seemed unbalanced. Prinze and McCullough decided to move, even though they had only lived in their house about a year. They found a new home a couple of blocks away that offered more security.

When Prinze moved out of his Tuluca Lake house, he gave it to his mother and grandmother. He had wanted to do this ever since he started in the business. It was his

## Uncomfortable Moments

Prinze found that, sometimes, filming movies was a pain. Some moments were merely embarrassing, such as his first on-screen kiss or his first on-screen love scene. *Wing Commander* provided another embarrassing moment. While making a military right face, Prinze whacked his head on a pipe and landed flat on his back, all with the cameras rolling.

In *I Know What You Did Last Summer* Prinze had to slide down a wet rope numerous times. His hands were torn up with third-degree rope burns. The next day he had to climb up nets to get into a boat. Even with bandages on his hands, salt water seeped into his cuts, making them even more painful.

During the filming of his various movies, Prinze has been dragged behind a boat through chilly water and dangled from wires while wearing a bulky space suit. He injured his shoulder throwing too many baseballs, and hurt his back in a fall. He was sprayed with soap that turned his skin crispy and was covered with mosquito bites. Still, his minor discomforts did not spoil his love of acting. "It's so much fun you pretend in every scene—I don't even need an alarm clock to wake up when I'm working 'cause I'm so excited."[8]

way of repaying them for taking care of him during his first eighteen years.

As he was enjoying the glow of success from *She's All That*, two more of Prinze's movies were released. They were both low-budget independent films that went directly to video. Although neither movie was considered a hit, they both added new dimensions to Prinze's acting.

For the most part, Prinze played characters that were wholesome, attractive young men. But real growth for an actor comes from taking on entirely different roles. Prinze accepted the challenge of playing an evil character in the movie *Vig*.

Prinze saw many opportunities for learning new things by accepting the part in *Vig*. Working with a British director and writer would expose him to different methods of filmmaking. The role also meant working with, and learning from, established actors Peter Falk, Timothy Hutton, and Lauren Holly.

In *Vig*, Prinze plays Tony, a hot-tempered drug addict who collects unpaid gambling debts for the mob. Tony is cruel and violent. He is the total opposite of Prinze's other roles.

"It was a tough character to shake when we were finished shooting for the day," Prinze said. "I was playing such a slimy person that I would literally have to go home at the end of the day and wash my hands to get the evil off of me."[9]

Signing on to play in *Vig* was a risky move for Prinze.

**A restaurant booth was the setting for this scene from *Sparkler*, which featured, from left, Freddie Prinze, Jr., Jamie Kennedy, and Steven Petrarca.**

Although it was not a financial success, he found the experience valuable. Prinze was especially impressed with Peter Falk. He considered Falk, who was seventy-two years old at the time, to be the best actor he had ever worked with. "He's just this awesome guy, who if you sit and talk to him it's like going to acting class for a year," Prinze said.[10]

The second movie, *Sparkler*, was a warm, offbeat comedy-drama. Park Overall played the part of Melba, a trailer park housewife who leaves her unfaithful husband. She goes to the local bar where she meets three young men, including Prinze's character, Brad. She assumes they are the three kings her psychic had told her to expect. The men are on their way to Las Vegas to win enough money to pay their rent. Melba decides to go with them. While she is gone, Melba's husband learns that she has won a sweepstakes. She only has seventy-two hours to appear in person to claim her million dollars.

Prinze's character, Brad, is a smart aleck trying to pass himself off as an agent. His character has no respect for women, which is not at all like Prinze himself.

As the new millennium approached, everything seemed to be going well for Prinze. He was making movies and winning awards. He had a beautiful new home. But an important part of his life was ending.

Kimberly McCullough was Prinze's first love. Their relationship had lasted for nearly four years. In the beginning they both assumed that it would lead to marriage. But their lives had changed over the years. Prinze's success in *I Know What You Did Last Summer* made him more in demand

> **"It was better for us to go our separate ways."**

for movie roles. He began spending extended periods of time on location filming back-to-back movies. This left little time to work on his relationship with McCullough. At the end of 1999, the couple parted.

Prinze did three movies in six months. "It cost me a

lot. . . . It cost me my girlfriend. . . . I'll never do that again," Prinze said.[11]

The breakup was difficult. McCullough had been an important part of Prinze's life. Then suddenly she was gone. "It was better for us to go our separate ways," Prinze said. "I'm still becoming a man and trying to figure out what this world is all about."[12]

In spite of the pain of seeing his relationship crumble, Prinze admitted that his years with McCullough had taught him a lot. "When you realize what went wrong, you become a better person. I learned from the mistakes we made."[13]

Prinze was left with an empty hole in his life. It could only be filled by a lot of work and a new love.

# 8

# Moving On

After his breakup with McCullough, Prinze threw himself into his work. That helped some, but he still missed having someone special in his life. The answer came from an unexpected source—his friend, Sarah Michelle Gellar. The two had become friends while working together on *I Know What You Did Last Summer* three years earlier. At that time, they each were involved with other people. Both of those relationships had ended.

One night, Prinze and Gellar planned to have dinner with a mutual friend. Their friend backed out at the last minute. "We decided to have dinner anyway and never looked back," said Gellar.[1]

Prinze joked later that Gellar had passed his food test. "In order for a girl to get a second date, I would take her to this restaurant and depending on how many courses she made it through that decided if she got a second date. Sarah made it through all seven courses, so I married her."[2]

Some people were surprised to see Prinze and Gellar as a couple. "When we were doing *I Know What You Did Last Summer*, I would have never thought of those two together," said the film's producer Neal H. Moritz. "I just found them to be so different. But when I see them out or at dinner, they just genuinely care so much about each other."[3]

Prinze gave Gellar credit for making him more creative. "She's inspiring and encouraging and very critical in a good way," he said. "That's how you know you're with a good person because they're able to bring you to the next level."[4]

Gellar admitted that she had also changed. "I went from reading Shakespeare to comic books," she joked. "I now play videogames and don't do my work ever because I'm too busy playing golf on the PlayStation."[5]

> "[Sarah's] inspiring and encouraging and very critical in a good way. That's how you know you're with a good person."

Prinze's love life was looking better. That was not the case with his character in *Down to You*, released in 2000. He played the part of Al Connelly, a college student in New York City. Al has a whirlwind romance with a fellow student. The two have

**Prinze, Jr., and Sarah Michelle Gellar walked the red carpet at the Teen Choice Awards in 2000.**

problems, separate, and move on to other partners. Later, they decide to give their relationship another try.

The object of Prinze's affection in the film was Imogen, played by Julia Stiles, from *10 Things I Hate About You*. Stiles enjoyed working with Prinze. "He is really goofy, and silly, and charming in real life, and he made me feel really comfortable so I could open up," she said.[6]

Selma Blair, who plays Cyrus in the movie, agreed. "He's the kind of guy who sees you to your car and makes sure everything's all right."[7]

Critics panned *Down to You*, but the film was a hit with Prinze's fans. It opened in the number one slot at the box office. Prinze went on to win the Teen Choice Award for "Choice Actor" for his role. He and Julia Stiles were nominated for "Choice Chemistry" and Stiles was nominated for "Choice Actress." The film was nominated for "Choice Comedy."

Prinze was not the only one to pick up an award at the Fox/*Seventeen* Teen Choice Awards in August 2000. Gellar won the award for "Choice Actress—TV" for her role in *Buffy the Vampire Slayer*.

Prinze's Choice Awards meant a lot more to him than being on *People* magazine's "50 Most Beautiful" lists in both 1999 and 2000, and their "Best Dressed" list for 2000. Although it was flattering to make the lists, Prinze could have done without the good-natured ribbing from his friends.

After making *She's All That* and *Down to You*, Prinze

made one more movie to fill out his trilogy of romantic comedies. In the first, the characters were in high school. The next two, *Down to You* and *Boys and Girls*, were set in college.

"These were three movies that I wanted to make for my generation," Prinze explained. "It was a goal of mine to create a video library of movies that kids could relate to, and now I'm finished."[8]

> "You have to learn how to talk all over again! . . . they don't tell you this until the day you're supposed to shoot with the braces."

In *Boys and Girls*, Prinze plays the part of Ryan, a dorky, structural engineering major with a logical plan for his life. He develops a friendship with Jennifer, played by Claire Forlani. Jennifer is the complete opposite of Ryan. She is majoring in Latin with no idea of what to do with it. The two become friends as they console each other over their romantic problems and create a few problems of their own.

One uncomfortable aspect of filming *Boys and Girls* involved Prinze's teeth. In the beginning of the movie, his character was a high school nerd. To look the part, Prinze had to be fitted for removable braces. He quickly discovered that talking with a mouthful of metal was not easy. "You have to learn how to talk all over again! Unfortunately they don't tell you this until the day you're supposed to shoot with the braces. There were like nine 's's' in one sentence, and I'm lisping."[9]

Prinze was also embarrassed by the dancing he had to do for the movie. For someone who counts tap dancing among his hobbies, it was embarrassing to have to dance like a dork. "Ryan's not supposed to know what's going on," Prinze said. "It's a cool song, I would've loved it, but it's not being honest to the character. I wish I didn't look like a putz dancing, though."[10]

After making *Boys and Girls*, Prinze retired from "teenage" roles. By that time, he was in his mid-twenties, too old to be convincing as a high school student. For his next movie, *Head Over Heels*, he plays the part of a twenty-seven-year-old fashion executive. The movie was directed by Mark Waters, who directed Prinze in *The House of Yes*.

*Head Over Heels* is another romantic comedy. It tells the story of a New York art restorer, Amanda Pierce (played by Monica Potter), who moves into an apartment with four supermodels. She falls in love with Jim Winston (Prinze), who lives next door. Amanda spends a lot of time watching Jim through the window. She becomes horrified when it appears that he murders a woman in his apartment. When the police cannot find a body, Amanda tries to find the missing woman.

Prinze joked about working with so many female costars. "You gotta know what it's like to work with six women and you're the only guy! They all think you're their little brother and they could do whatever they want. Whether it's trying to give you Indian burns or see how strong they are."[11]

*Head Over Heels* was Prinze's thirteenth movie, including the two made for television. He had played all kinds of roles, but not the one he really wanted to play. He had grown up reading comic books, an interest that continued into adulthood. One of his favorite super-heroes is Spider-Man. "In the comics he and I looked exactly the same. He was a kid who didn't fit in, then got this power and really didn't fit in, but he did good with it."[12]

Prinze always hoped that he would get to play Spider-Man if a movie were ever made about the superhero. As soon as he heard that one was being planned, he talked to director Sam Raimi. "I thought I would get that movie based on what people told me and the delusion that I created," Prinze said.[13]

> "I thought I would get that movie based on what people told me and the delusion that I created."

Unfortunately, Raimi and Prinze had different ideas as to how the character should be played. In the end, the part went to Tobey Maguire. Prinze was very disappointed at first. Later he realized that Maguire's Spider-Man fit better with the way Raimi wanted the part played. "Tobey did a fantastic job and I would have done it very differently," Prinze said.[14]

Prinze did not let his disappointment get him down for long. He knew he had to move on to other projects. A movie came along that gave him a chance to fight crime, but not as a superhero. Instead of coming from a comic book, his next role was snatched from one of Prinze's favorite Saturday morning cartoons. This time, one of his costars would be a large talking dog.

The movie *Scooby-Doo–Where Are You?* is a live-action version of the popular *Scooby-Doo* cartoons. It seemed like a perfect fit for a lifelong fan like Prinze. Over the years he had collected copies of every *Scooby-Doo* cartoon ever made—all 340 of them. He even has a Scooby-Doo bowling ball.

Surprisingly, Prinze was hesitant to do the movie at first. He did not like the idea of having a live-action version of the well-known cartoon. Then Gellar convinced him to read the script. When Prinze saw how funny the script was, he talked to his agent about auditioning for the role.

Prinze played Fred Jones, the arrogant leader of the mystery-solving team. Gellar played the stylish damsel-in-distress, Daphne. The part of Shaggy was played by Prinze's friend and frequent costar, Matthew Lillard. Filling out the Mystery, Inc., foursome is Linda Cardellini as Velma, the brains of the group.

In the film, the Mystery Inc. gang reunites on Spooky Island after having gone their separate ways two

## The Dog That Wasn't There

When filming movies, the actors must respond to the other people in the scene. But how do you interact with a large dog whose computer-generated image will not be added until the filming is done? Several techniques were used in making *Scooby-Doo* to help the actors know where Scooby was. Sometimes a big "X" was the only thing needed to mark his location. At other times, a stick with a dog's head on it was used. For more active scenes, an actual person was needed to fill in for Scooby. A short actor was dressed in a dog suit so the cast could see exactly what Scooby was doing.

When Scooby was frightened, he often jumped on someone. To help the actors react realistically, the visual-effects people used a large bag filled with sawdust and buckshot. They threw the bag on the person targeted for Scooby's frightened leap.

Although the actors could not see Scooby, they could hear him. Neil Fanning, who supplied Scooby's voice for the movie, barked his lines.

**Freddie Prinze, Jr., had to repeatedly bleach his hair blonde to play Fred in the movie *Scooby-Doo*.**

years earlier. The proprietor of an amusement park calls the team in to help him with a dilemma. Perfectly normal teenage visitors are turning into zombies. The foursome is forced to work together to solve the mystery.

*Scooby-Doo* began filming in February of 2001 in Queensland on Australia's Gold Coast. It was a very long shoot. Most of Prinze's films were shot in ten weeks or so. This one took nearly six months. That was a long time to be away from home. The only thing that made the shoot bearable was having Sarah there with him.

> *"Every week I had my brown hair bleached blonde."*

Being stranded in Australia was not the only downside to filming *Scooby-Doo*. Prinze also had to adjust to living life as a blonde. "Every week I had my brown hair bleached blonde. We were there for six months, and at the wrap of the movie, my hair was like steel wool. The only thing I could do was shave my head bald, and let the hair grow back."[15]

Although Prinze did not enjoy being in Australia for such a long time, he made the best of it. One memorable night, he did something that would change his life.

# Romance, Dogs, and Baseball

The highlight of Prinze and Gellar's time in Australia had nothing to do with filming *Scooby-Doo*. One April night in 2001, Prinze treated Gellar to a romantic dinner. He presented her with a princess-cut diamond engagement ring that he had helped design. By that time, the two had been dating for over a year. They knew they wanted to be together for the rest of their lives.

On the surface, Prinze and Gellar seem like an odd couple. She is an early bird while he is a night owl. He is hooked on comics while she reads selections from Oprah's Book Club. Clarissa Cruz of *Entertainment Weekly* described the two as being "as mismatched as one of Shaggy's grilled-eggplant-and-chocolate-syrup sandwiches."[1]

In reality, the two are very compatible. They both shun Hollywood's wild life and fiercely guard their privacy. They both have an interest in food. Prinze likes to cook it, and Gellar likes to eat it. Even their upbringings have some similarities. They both are only children raised by single mothers. Gellar's parents divorced when she was seven. She had little contact with her father after that. Like Prinze, Gellar remained close to her mother, Rosellen, a former nursery-school teacher.

Gellar also felt out of place in high school. Most of the other students at the Professional Children's School in New York were wealthy. Gellar and her mother lived on a tight budget. She paid for school with a partial scholarship and the money she earned from making commercials.

*"Years ago, I wouldn't have been ready to get married. Now I'm really ready. He's my best friend."*
—*Sarah Michelle Gellar*

A few days after Prinze's proposal, the happy couple made their formal announcement at her twenty-fourth birthday party. "We're the perfect example of timing," Gellar said. "We knew each other for years, but we were in different places. Years ago, I wouldn't have been ready to get married. Now I'm really ready. He's my best friend."[2]

No sooner were they engaged than the couple had to separate—at least temporarily. Gellar headed back to Los Angeles to her starring role on *Buffy*. Prinze had to remain in Australia to finish filming *Scooby-Doo*. He had a hard time being away from his fiancée. "Freddie always wanted to fly home to hang out with Sarah, but I wouldn't let him," Lillard said.[3]

The rest of the cast benefited from Prinze's loneliness. To keep his mind off Gellar, he often cooked for his friends. He was relieved when filming wrapped up and he could get back to California.

At the beginning of 2002, Prinze and Gellar each put their houses up for sale. At that time, Prinze owned a four-thousand-square-foot villa. It had two master suites, tennis courts, a swimming pool, and a two-bedroom guest house. Gellar's home came with four bedrooms, seven bathrooms, a spa, and an outdoor kitchen. The couple bought a $3 million five-bedroom home in the San Fernando Valley. Prinze insisted that the new house have a large kitchen.

Prinze and Gellar are happiest just hanging out together at home. Their favorite companions are their dogs, Tyson and Thor. Walking dogs and doing grocery shopping may not sound like a wild life, but that is the way the couple wants it. They often entertain friends at home. "Freddie's an amazing chef," Gellar said. "And I wash a mean dish."[4]

As a celebrity couple, keeping their relationship private is often difficult. "Sarah and I work because we don't talk about our relationship [to the press]," Prinze said. "We're able to deal with the challenges that every couple deals with. And ours aren't unique. But we mainly work because we stay very private."[5]

As much as they try to keep their lives out of public view, it does not always work. As with most celebrities, Prinze and Gellar are often the target of the paparazzi. For the most part, they put up with the cameras. But Prinze thought one photographer had gone too far. It happened the day Prinze took Gellar to the Forest Lawn cemetery to visit his father's grave. A photographer took pictures of the couple and sold them to a tabloid. Along with the photographs was a fictitious story complete with quotes that Prinze and Gellar had supposedly said. Prinze was upset that someone had invaded his privacy to that extent. Now when they are out, he checks more closely to see if they are being followed.[6]

In August 2001, Prinze's next movie, *Summer Catch*, was released. Filming the sports movie allowed Prinze to combine his love of acting with his love of baseball. He plays the part of Ryan Dunne, a young man from the working class with a superior pitching arm. Ryan is one of the rare local boys who make it into the Cape Cod Baseball League. The league showcases the best college baseball players and gives them a chance to be seen by major-league scouts.

Prinze and his friend, Matthew Lillard, teamed up again for the filming of *Summer Catch*. Lillard plays Ryan's buddy, Billy Brubaker. Ryan's summer also includes a romance with Tenley Parrish, played by

Jessica Biel. Tenley is a rich graduate from Vassar who spends her summers in Cape Cod with her family.

*Summer Catch* is Biel's first leading role in a movie. Prinze made sure that she felt at ease on the set. "He was almost brotherly, making sure I was comfortable, okay with the lines, the wardrobe. My nervousness fell away when I realized all the support I had around me," Biel said.[7] She went on to describe her costar as "a gentleman and a goofball."[8]

In one way, Prinze's character is different from Prinze himself. Dunne has a temper and goes into a rage when anything goes wrong. Prinze is the type that gets quiet when he gets upset. He would rather be by himself until he figures things out.

> *"I felt that understanding the character meant understanding how to pitch."*

Before filming began, Prinze had to be trained as a pitcher. "It would have been easy to grab a double and just let him do everything, but I felt that understanding the character meant understanding how to pitch," said Prinze.[9]

The actor's first pitching experience had involved standing behind a pitching machine as a youngster in Little League. It was not quite the training he needed to look like a pro. The studio hired three pitching coaches to prepare Prinze for the role. "That was my favorite

**Brian Dennehy, playing a coach, has a word with Freddie Prinze, Jr.'s character in** *Summer Catch.* **To the left of Dennehy is Prinze, Jr.'s friend, Matthew Lillard, who played the team's catcher in the movie.**

part of making the film," he said. "They gave me some of the best pitching scouts and pitching coaches in the country, and actual baseball pitchers to make sure that my pitch was perfect."[10]

The coaches put Prinze through rigorous training using the same techniques they used for the pros. Some days he would have to throw eighty or ninety pitches. "My arm felt like it was eight feet long and made out of Jell-O," Prinze remembered.[11]

Although they did not use a stunt double for Prinze's

pitching, he did insist on someone else taking his place for one scene. In the film, Ryan's friends play a practical joke on him. They steal his clothes while he is camped out in the park. The only thing he can find to put on is girl's orange thong underwear. The "no nudity" clause in Prinze's contract saved him from filming the embarrassing incident.

Using a body double for the scene in *Summer Catch* did not keep readers of *CosmoGIRL!* from naming Prinze their "Sexiest Man of the Year" in 2001. According to the magazine, it was not Prinze's good looks that won him the title. "It's that this is a guy who's always thinking about others, about the way the world works, about how he can make himself a better person. That quality is way more attractive than his looks could ever be. He's a real guy—the kind you'd love to just chill with."[12]

On June 8, 2002, *Scooby-Doo* was released. As with many of Prinze's films, *Scooby-Doo* failed to impress most critics. However, Prinze's fans did not let him down. Once again, his movie was number one at the box office, earning $54 million its opening weekend. *Scooby-Doo* went on to gross more than $275 million worldwide.[13]

Many actors get upset with poor reviews. Prinze never paid much attention to reviews, whether they were good or bad. "If I read a great review about me, I don't care and it doesn't make me feel particularly good about myself, because I already do. On the other hand, if I read a BAD review I don't care either, because it doesn't change the way I feel about my work."[14]

Gellar, on the other hand, had a hard time enduring the harsh words of reviewers. Prinze tried to help her put things in perspective. "*Scooby-Doo* isn't for reviewers. We're not making it for them," he told her.[15]

Gellar finally realized that he was right. "When all these children came up to me to say, '*Scooby-Doo* is my favorite movie,' that was great," Gellar admitted. "But for a weird time in between, I took everything really personally."[16]

*Scooby-Doo* was a hit with teens. Gellar won the Teen Choice Award for "Choice Actress, Comedy." Prince and Matthew Lillard were both nominated for "Choice Actor, Comedy." Additionally, Prinze and Gellar were nominated for "Choice Chemistry."

Although the couple did not win the Teen Choice Award for their chemistry, they certainly did not lack it offscreen. While refusing to answer any questions about their wedding plans, they were secretly preparing for the big event. They tied the knot in the Mexican resort town of Costa Careyes on September 1, 2002. The couple kept the date and place a secret from everyone but friends and family. As a result, their ceremony had little interference from the paparazzi. Interference from Mother Nature, however, was not as easy to control.

During their wedding weekend, Hurricane Hernan was churning up the ocean three hundred miles away. Storms spreading out from the hurricane battered the

Freddie Prinze, Jr., and Sarah Michelle Gellar were married in Costa
Careyes, Mexico.

## Prinze's Bride

Sarah Michelle Gellar's career began at age four when an agent spotted her in a New York restaurant. Her first job was filming a commercial for Burger King that attacked McDonald's by name. "McDonalds were so outraged, they sued Burger King and named me in the lawsuit. I wasn't allowed to eat there. It was tough, because, when you're a little kid, McDonald's is where all your friends have their birthday parties."[17]

Sarah is intelligent and hardworking. She graduated with honors from New York's Professional Children's School at age fifteen. In addition to school and acting, she competed in figure skating. At one time she was ranked third in the New York State regional competition.

A big break came in 1993 when Gellar was cast on the soap opera *All My Children*. Two years later, she won a Daytime Emmy for her role on the show. Gellar moved to California in 1996 to pursue a career in television and movies.

Gellar's biggest break came when she won the lead of the TV series *Buffy the Vampire Slayer*. Movie roles followed, including *I Know What You Did Last Summer*, where she met her future husband.

resort with high winds and rain. The couple did not let the unpleasant weather dampen their spirits. They scrapped their plans for a beach wedding and moved the ceremony to a villa in town.

About sixty friends and family members attended the ceremony. Celebrity guests included Shannen Doherty (*North Shore*), Wilmer Valderrama (*That '70s Show*), and Dulé Hill (*The West Wing*). The wedding was officiated by the couple's close friend, choreographer, and film director Adam Shankman (*Hairspray*). Shankman had worked as a choreographer on *She's All That* and *Buffy the Vampire Slayer*. He became ordained on an Internet site in order to preside over the nondenominational service. "It's a crazy honor," Shankman said of the unusual request.[18]

Her mother gave away the beautiful bride, wearing a gown designed by Vera Wang. A dinner reception was followed by an evening of dancing.

The hurricane was not the only surprise nature provided that weekend. The next day an earthquake measuring 4.6 on the Richter scale rocked the area. "Earthquake? Hurricane? Hey, I think it's a great way to start," said family friend Ron DiBlasio. "All of those bigger-than-life natural events can only bode well for the marriage."[19]

Several months after her marriage, Sarah Michelle Gellar announced another big change in her life. For seven years she had starred in her television series, *Buffy the Vampire Slayer*. Near the end of the seventh season,

Gellar announced her plans to leave the show. She worried that viewers would blame her for ending the show. In reality, unofficial plans had already been made to bring it to a close.

*Buffy* had survived a temporary slump in ratings a year earlier. When its popularity returned, Gellar felt that the time was right for her to leave. She announced her decision in an emotional interview with *Entertainment Weekly*. "You always worry about being the show that's been on too long—especially when you're a cult hit. This is how I want to go out—on top, at our best." Gellar explained. "I was 18 when I started the show; I'm 26. I'm married. I never see my husband."[20]

Gellar was not the only one to make changes after the wedding. Prinze was also ready to try some new things.

# 10

# Branching Out

Many of Prinze's later movies did not do well at the box office. He decided to step back for awhile. Guest appearances on two popular television shows kept him in front of the cameras. In 2002, he played an overly sensitive male nanny on the popular sitcom *Friends*. He later guest starred on *Boston Legal* as the son of Denny Crane (William Shatner), the eccentric head of a law firm. Prinze returned for guest roles in 2005 and 2006. He was also a frequent guest on the talk show circuit.

Early in 2003, Prinze took on a new challenge. He had acted in movies and television, but never onstage. That changed when he accepted a role in a London theater. He was part of the cast for the long-running play *This Is Our Youth*. Also in the cast were Chris Klein of *American Pie* and Heather Burns from *You've Got Mail*. Prinze played a spoiled teen who stole fifteen thousand dollars from his father. He used the money for drugs and alcohol.

Acting in front of a live audience was a new experience for Prinze. He enjoyed the added control he had over his performance. "If you get it wrong one night, you can make it better the next," he explained.[1]

Prinze had never been to London before. February may not have been the best time for his first visit. When asked about his first impression of the city, Prinze replied "It's cold, it's very cold. Understand this, I'm a Puerto Rican and God didn't equip us for this kind of cold. Staying here for two months is going to be very interesting."[2] He also had to get used to people driving on the left side of the road.

Soon after Prinze arrived home from London, he and Gellar left for Canada to film *Scooby-Doo 2: Monsters Unleashed*. In this sequel, the members of Mystery, Inc. attend the opening of the Coolsville Museum of Criminology. One exhibit displays costumes from the villains the group has dealt with in the past. Someone steals the costumes and brings them back to life. It is up to Mystery Inc. to recapture them.

*Scooby-Doo 2* opened in April 2004. Like the original, *Scooby-Doo 2* was the weekend's number one movie. However, the film earned less than $30 million its first weekend.[3] That number fell far below the opening weekend for the first *Scooby-Doo* movie two years earlier. Many critics felt that *Scooby-Doo 2* was the better movie. They guessed that it had been hurt by the poor reviews of the original. The results caused Warner Brothers to cancel its plans for *Scooby-Doo 3*.

By the time *Scooby-Doo 2* was released, Prinze was twenty-seven years old. Again, he felt ready to branch out into something new. As a child, Prinze had used his imagination to create a make-believe world. Now he wanted to put the same creativity to work as a writer. He began by penning an episode for the science-fiction television series *Mutant X*. Being a fan of the series made it easy to write his episode. He enjoyed being able to create the kind of dialogue that he wished he had gotten in his movies. Prinze's episode, titled "One Step Closer," aired in April 2003.

The opportunity to try scriptwriting came about through Prinze's friendship with Seth Howard, creative executive producer of the *Mutant X* television series. "We were talking about the show, the things we liked and the things we didn't," Prinze recalled. "Seth said, 'If you're so smart, write an episode.' And I said, 'OK.' They gave me pretty much total freedom to write my story within their world, and that's what I did."[4]

"He is a tremendous writer and I look forward to him writing another one for Season 3," Howard said. "His take on our characters is refreshing and exciting.

> *"They gave me pretty much total freedom to write my story within their world, and that's what I did."*

He's a real class act and don't be surprised if he becomes more known for his writing in the future."[5]

Prinze had made a name for himself in acting and now writing. But he was always aware that he shared his famous name with his father. Many years earlier, he had made a graveside pledge to bring his father's name back up to the top. Finally, the day arrived when Prinze could see his father get the recognition he deserved.

On December 14, 2004, the late Freddie Prinze, Sr., received a star on the Hollywood Walk of Fame. He was honored for his talent as a comedian and his contribution to the entertainment industry. As only the second Latino to star in a television series, he had inspired other Latino stars. One was George Lopez who went on to star in his own sitcom, *The George Lopez Show*. It was Lopez who nominated the late comedian and sponsored his star. "He called them and said, 'How does Woody Woodpecker have a star and Freddie Prinze doesn't?'" Prinze, Jr., said.[6]

It was hard for Prinze, Jr., to control his emotions as he spoke at the ceremony to unveil his father's star. "I always get overwhelmed when it comes to speaking about my father," the twenty-eight-year-old told the crowd. "To see the respect from the people in L.A. and New York where my father was from brings tears to my eyes. To walk by and see his name on this star, wow!"[7]

George Lopez was not the only Latino to benefit from Prinze, Sr.'s success. Like his father, Freddie Prinze, Jr., had the chance to make his mark on

Actor Freddie Prinze, Jr., and his mother, Kathy Cochran, have an emotional moment while looking at a replica plaque, as his late father and her husband, Freddie Prinze, Sr., was honored during ceremonies unveiling Prinze's star on the Hollywood Walk of Fame, in Los Angeles, California, on December 14, 2004.

television. In 2005, he had a sitcom of his own called *Freddie*. Prinze was very involved in the show. In addition to playing the lead, he also helped create, write, and produce the show. The twenty-nine-year-old became ABC's youngest executive producer at that time.

In *Freddie*, Prinze plays a bachelor working as a chef. His life changes when he takes in several of his female relatives who are having financial problems. His new housemates include his grandmother, sister, niece, and sister-in-law.

## Birth of a Series

As with any creative venture, a series such as *Freddie* begins with an idea. Each fall, hundreds of producers and writers pitch their ideas to television executives. The networks arrange to have scripts written for the best ideas. If a script shows promise, a pilot, or test episode, will be filmed. Pilots give a much clearer picture of whether a show will work or not.

Developing new shows is expensive. It can cost around $3 million to make a pilot for a half-hour comedy. A pilot for an hour drama could run $6 million. Pilots are usually shown to focus groups to judge their reaction. Most are not shown to a national audience.

If a show makes it through all these levels and is good enough to attract sponsors, it is put on the schedule. Out of about a hundred pilots that are made each year, only thirty or so will make it on to network television. Of these, only a few will go on to become hit shows.

In some ways, the show reflected Prinze's own life. Similar to his character in *Freddie*, Prinze grew up surrounded by women. "I was raised by my mother and my grandmother, I spent Christmases in Puerto Rico with my other grandmother and her sisters, and some summers I was in California with my godmother and two godsisters. Half my family is Puerto Rican and the other half is Italian."[8]

The grandmother on the show spoke only Spanish. Her lines came with English subtitles. This was a nod to Prinze's own grandmother, Maria Pruetzel, in Puerto Rico. She used to tell him, "When you're in France, you speak French, when you're in America, you speak English, but when you speak to God, you speak Spanish."[9]

Prinze gave Lopez much of the credit for his new show. Lopez encouraged Prinze to develop *Freddie*. He also agreed to let his producer, Bruce Helford, work on both shows.

Wearing three hats—as coproducer, cowriter, and actor—was a challenge for Prinze. "Writing and taking notes and rewriting and casting and trying to make sure small things like having the right song for a club scene: All that stuff is so much work, I don't really have time to think about anything in my 'spare time' except to act," he said of his fifteen-hour workdays.[10]

Prinze found that working on a weekly television series was much different from filming a movie. Movies are shot a scene at a time. The dialogue can be learned in smaller chunks. Television is more immediate.

*Freddie* cast members included, from left, Chloe Suazo, Mädchen Amick, Freddie Prinze, Jr., Brian Austin Green, Jacqueline Obradors, and Jenny Gago. This picture was taken on the set of the show at Warner Brothers Studios in Burbank, California, on January 23, 2006.

"You're doing an entire play a week, and the amount of information that goes in your head and comes out of your mouth in a five-day period is insane, and it doesn't let me rest. And I like that. I gotta keep pushing myself forward," Prinze said.[11]

Prinze surprised Jenny Gago, who played the part of the grandmother on *Freddie*. "I imagined a very young Hollywood player-playboy. What I found was a very deep well, a very charismatic young man who has a very big heart and wonderful huge dreams that he's making happen."[12]

Prinze hoped his show would run for several years. It made it through its first season of twenty-two shows,

but did not get renewed for a second season. Not having his show renewed for another season was a big disappointment for Prinze. But he had suffered disappointments before and was not going to let this one get him down.

On March 16, 2006, Prinze was once again on hand to accept an award for his father. At that time, AOL and Warner Brothers were launching a new television lineup called *In2TV*. The new venture put thousands of classic TV shows from the past forty years on the Web. One of the shows in the collection was *Chico and the Man*, starring the late Freddie Prinze, Sr.

A gala event was held to launch the new programming.

Freddie Prinze, Sr., was honored with the first In2TV Influencer Award. He was recognized for his "ground-breaking contributions and legacy as a Latino actor."[13]

"This is a fitting tribute to a man whose career helped open doors for Latinos in entertainment," Prinze, Jr., said as he accepted the award for his father. "I'm sure he'd be humbled by this recognition."[14]

AOL and Warner Brothers further honored the late comedian. They established the Freddie Prinze Scholarship at the University of Southern California School of Cinema-Television. The scholarship goes to a graduate student who uses his or her creative talents to promote Latinos in television.

Although Prinze had turned to television, he still had movies waiting to come out. He and Gellar both supplied the voices for the animated movie *Happily N'Ever After*, released in January 2007. Prinze was seen on-screen again with Alec Baldwin in *Brooklyn Rules*. It was released in a limited number of theaters in April 2007. *Jack & Jill vs. the World* and the animated film *Delgo* were released in 2008.

The disappointment of having his series, *Freddie*, canceled after one season did not spoil Prinze's interest in television. In the spring of 2007, he starred in the pilot of the comedy series *Atlanta*. As with most pilots, it was uncertain at the time whether the show would make it into the weekly lineup.

Prinze is also branching out with more work behind the camera. He and childhood friend Conrad Jackson formed a production company called Hunga Rican Entertainment. Together they produced a suspense thriller, *Manslaughter*. Prinze is the executive producer and has a cameo role in the film.

Even though Gellar and Prinze are busy with their various projects, they still make their marriage a top priority. The couple works hard to arrange their schedules so they can spend time together. It is a policy that is not always easy to follow. In the summer of 2007, Gellar turned down the chance to star in a movie with Robert De Niro and Michelle Pfeiffer. Filming *Stardust* would have required Gellar to spend a great deal of time in Scotland. "I turned it down because it was Freddie's turn in New York. I would have loved to have done it— are you kidding? But it was Freddie's turn," she said.[15]

There is one real-life role that Prinze has looked forward to for a long time. He wants to be a father. "For a young boy to never have had a father—you create an image in your mind of what the perfect father would be, and for better or worse, I don't have any choice but to be that for my child," he said.[16]

Friends of the couple feel certain that they will make good parents. Gellar is always willing to watch her friends' kids. On the *Scooby* set, she and Prinze enjoyed playing with the children of their director, Raja Gosnell. "Sarah would sit with my kids and play and sing. Freddie would show my older son wrestling holds. They'd be amazing parents," Gosnell said.[17]

Prinze has come a long way since the day the

eighteen-year-old visited his father's grave to share the joy of his first job. With his hand on the plaque, he had expressed his hope that he would make his father proud. Most would agree that his hope has been fulfilled.

Freddie Prinze, Jr., succeeded in a competitive field because of his hard work, his desire to keep improving, and his refusal to give up. More than that, he has grown up to be a good person with strong values. Given his young age, there is no limit to what he can accomplish in the future. Judging from past experience, he will give each goal no less than 100 percent of his effort. What father would not be proud of that?

# Entertainment Career

## FILMS

1996   *To Gillian on Her 37th Birthday*

1997   *The House of Yes*

       *I Know What You Did Last Summer*

       *Sparkler*

1998   *I Still Know What You Did Last Summer*

       *Vig*

1999   *She's All That*

       *Wing Commander*

2000   *Down to You*

       *Boys and Girls*

2001   *Head Over Heels*

       *Summer Catch*

2002   *Scooby-Doo*

2004   *Scooby-Doo 2: Monsters Unleashed*

2005   *Shooting Gallery (video)*

2006   *Shark Bait (voice)*

2007   *Happily N'Ever After (voice)*

       *Brooklyn Rules*

       *New York City Serenade*

2008 *Jack & Jill vs. the World*

*Delgo (voice)*

## TELEVISION

1995 *Family Matters (1 episode)*

1996 *Too Soon for Jeff*

1997 *Detention: The Siege at Johnson High*

2002 *Frasier (1 episode)*

*Friends (1 episode)*

2003 *Kim Possible: A Stitch in Time (voice)*

2004 *Boston Legal (3 episodes 2004–2006)*

2005 *Freddie (22 episodes 2005–2006)*

2006 *The George Lopez Show (1 episode)*

## WRITER

2003 *Mutant X (1 episode)*

2006 *Freddie (12 episodes)*

## PRODUCER

2005 *Freddie (12 episodes)*

2007 *Manslaughter*

# Chronology

**1976**—Freddie Prinze, Jr., is born in Los Angeles on March 8 to Freddie Prinze, Sr., and Kathy Cochran.

**1977**—Father (Freddie Prinze, Sr.) dies January 29 of a self-inflicted gunshot wound.

**1980**—Freddie Prinze, Jr., moves to Albuquerque, New Mexico with his mother.

**1994**—Graduates from La Cueva High School and moves to Los Angeles to pursue acting career; gets first acting role on *Family Matters*.

**1995**—Plays title role in ABC Afterschool Special, *Too Soon for Jeff*; wins role in first feature movie, *To Gillian on Her 37th Birthday*.

**1996**—Begins dating Kimberly McCullough; films dark comedy *The House of Yes*; selected as "Mr. Golden Globe" for the Golden Globe awards ceremony.

**1997**—Appears in television movie *Detention: The Siege at Johnson High*, and teen horror film, *I Know What You Did Last Summer*; wins Blockbuster Entertainment Award for his supporting role; *The House of Yes* released.

**1998**—*I Still Know What You Did Last Summer* is released; films *Wing Commander* and *She's All That*; *Vig* is released to video.

**1999**—*She's All That* is the number one movie at the box office its opening weekend; wins three Teen Choice awards; *Wing Commander* and *Sparkler* are released; breaks up with McCullough.

**2000**—Stars in *Down to You* and *Boys and Girls*; begins dating Sarah Michelle Gellar; named on *People* magazine's lists of "50 Most Beautiful People of the World," and "Best Dressed."

**2001**—Stars in *Head Over Heels* and *Summer Catch*; goes to Australia to film *Scooby-Doo*; becomes engaged to Gellar; named "Sexiest Man of the Year" by *CosmoGIRL!* magazine.

**2002**—Marries Sarah Michelle Gellar on September 1; *Scooby-Doo* is released.

**2003**—Appears on the London stage in *This Is Our Youth*; writes script for one episode of *Mutant-X* television series

**2004**—*Scooby-Doo 2: Monsters Unleashed* is released; speaks at ceremony to unveil his father's star on Hollywood Walk of Fame.

**2005**—Serves as cocreator, coproducer, cowriter, and star of ABC comedy *Freddie*.

**2006**—Films *New York City Serenade* and *Jack & Jill vs. the World*; accepted first "In2TV Influencer Award" for his father.

**2007**—Produces *Manslaughter* and films pilot for TV series *Atlanta*.

**2008**—*Jack & Jill vs. the World* and animated film *Delgo* are scheduled for release.

# Chapter Notes

## CHAPTER 1. A NEW STAR ON THE HORIZON

1. "Eerie Serendipity," Studio Briefing, *The Internet Movie Database (IMDb)*, January 29, 1999, <http://www.imdb.com/news/sb/1999-01-29> (October 26, 2007).
2. *"She's All That,"* Box Office Mojo, n.d., <http://www.boxofficemojo.com/movies/?id=shesallthat.htm> (November 3, 2007).
3. Bob Ivry, "Don't Confuse '*She's All That*' Star Freddie Prinze Jr. With His Father," *The Record*, January 25, 1999, p. G5.
4. "AOL Chat Transcript," *AOL*, January 27, 2001, <http://www.ilovefreddie.com/transcript_aolchat01.html> (October 26, 2007).
5. "The 50 Most Beautiful People in the World 1999—Freddie Prinze Jr.," *People*, May 10, 1999, p. 197.
6. Todd Gold, "Steady Freddie," *Rollingstone.com*, August 23, 2001, <http://www.rollingstone.com/news/story/5932918/steady_freddie> (October 28, 2007).
7. "Eerie Serendipity."

## CHAPTER 2. FATHERLESS

1. Maria Pruetzel and John A. Barbour, *The Freddie Prinze Story* (Kalamazoo, Mich.: Master's Press, 1978), p. 218.
2. Daniel Bernardi, "Freddie Prinze, US Actor," *MBC-Museum of Broadcast Communications*, n.d., <http://www.museum.tv/archives/etv/P/htmlP/prinzefredd/prinzefredd.htm> (October 28, 2007).
3. Ibid.

4. Pruetzel and Barbour, p. 93.
5. Dotson Rader, "Nothing Could Stop Me but Me," *Parade*, August 2001, <http://freddieprinzejr.com/articles_parade01.htm> (October 16, 2007).
6. J. D. Reed and Marc Ballon, "Fresh Prinze," *People*, November 18, 1996, p. 135.
7. Marc Shapiro, *Freddie Prinze Jr.* (New York: Berkley Publishing Group, 1999), p. 38.
8. "Ten Burning Questions for Freddie Prinze Jr.," *ESPN.COM Page 2*, August 2001, <http://espn.go.com/page2/s/questions/prinze.html> (October 16, 2007).
9. Reed and Ballon.
10. Allan Johnson, "Only Lately has Freddie Prinze Jr. Begun Getting Over His Father's Death," *Chicago Tribune*, January 27, 1999, Section: Tempo, p. 1.
11. Stephen Rebello, "Freddie Prinze," *Movieline*, March 1999, <http://www.ilovefreddie.com/article_movieline99.html> (October 28, 2007).
12. Rader.
13. David A. Keeps, "Prince Freddie," *Teen People*, June/July 2001, p. 84.

## CHAPTER 3. THE OUTSIDER

1. Deborah Baer, "Prinze Charming," *CosmoGIRL!*, September 2001, p 124.
2. Stephen Schaefer, "Freddie Jr. and the Man," *Boston Herald*, January 28, 1999, p. 051.
3. "The Rosie O'Donnell Show (transcript)," *JennaAngelfire*, January 13, 1999, <http://www.angelfire.com/me/JennaAngelfire/rosie.html> (October 29, 2007).
4. Allan Johnson, "Only Lately has Freddie Prinze Jr. Begun Getting Over His Father's Death," *Chicago Tribune*, January 27, 1999, Section: Tempo, p. 1.
5. "The Rosie O' Donnell Show (transcript)."

6. "Freddie on the Tonight Show With Jay Leno (transcript)," *JennaAngelfire*, December 7, 1998, <http://www. angelfire.com/me/JennaAngelfire/TonightShow.html> (October 17, 2007).

7. David A. Keeps, "Prince Freddie," *Teen People*, June/July 2001, p. 84.

8. Marc Shapiro, *Freddie Prinze Jr.* (New York: Berkley Publishing Group, 1999), p. 48.

9. Joshua Mooney, "Prinze Charming Freddie Prinze Jr. Doesn't Believe in Fairy Tales, but the Talented Young Actor Appears Headed for a Happy Ending," *The Fresno Bee*, January 22, 1999, p. E12.

10. Shapiro, p. 51.

## CHAPTER 4. RISKY MOVE

1. Marc Shapiro, *Freddie Prinze Jr.* (New York: Berkley Publishing Group, 1999), p. 53.

2. "Answer the Questions! Freddie Prinze Jr.; I am my Own Male Role Model," *The Independent on Sunday*, (London), February 9, 2003, <http://www.findarticles.com/p/ articles/mi_qn4159/is_20030209/ai_n12734673/print> (October 28, 2007).

3. "Freddie on the Tonight Show With Jay Leno (transcript)," *JennaAngelfire*, December 7, 1998, <http://www. angelfire.com/me/JennaAngelfire/TonightShow.html> (October 28, 2007).

4. "Late Show with David Letterman (transcript)," *FreddiePrinzeJr.com*, June 2002, <http://www. freddieprinzejr.com/transcript_letterman02.htm> (October 16, 2007).

5. Dotson Rader, "Nothing Could Stop Me but Me," *Parade*, August, 2001, <http://freddieprinzejr.com/articles_ parade01.htm> (October 16, 2007).

6. Shapiro, p. 56.

7. Ibid.

8. Gill Pringle, "Freddie Prinze Jr.," *Dolly Magazine* (Australia), January 2002, <http://www.freddieprinzejr. com/articles_dolly02.htm> (October 28, 2007).

9. Ibid.

10. Ibid.

11. "Biography for Freddie Prinze Jr.," *The Internet Movie Database (IMDb)*, n.d., <http://www.imdb.com/name/ nm0005327/bio> (October 29, 2007).

12. J. D. Reed and Marc Ballon, "Fresh Prinze," *People*, November 18, 1996, p. 135.

13. Greg Adkins, et. al., "Freddie Prinze, Jr.," *People*, December 27, 2004, p 30.

14. Kevin Donegan, "Study Finds More Latinos, Fewer Asians on Prime-time TV," *Common Dreams News Center*, April 20, 2004, <http://www.commondreams.org/cgi-bin/print. cgi?file=/news2004/0420-15.htm> (October 28, 2007).

15. Eric Deggans, "Freddie Prinze, Jr.," *Hispanic*, September 2005, p. 19.

16. Shapiro, p. 77.

17. "The Tonight Show With Jay Leno (transcript)."

## CHAPTER 5. GROWTH SPURT

1. "The Facts of Life," *Soap Opera Magazine*, © 1998, <http://romanticsgarden.com/kimberly/articles1.htm> (October 17, 2007).

2. Dennis Hensley, "Prinze Charming," *Seventeen*, February 2000, p. 98.

3. Ibid.

4. Ibid.

5. "Freddie Prinze," *AOL's Entertainment Asylum Transcript* (online chat), March 11, 1999, *JennaAngelfire*, <http:// www.angelfire.com/mi/JennaAngelfire/aolasly.html> (October 28, 2007).

6. J. D. Reed and Marc Ballon, "Fresh Prinze," *People*, November 18, 1996, p. 135.

7. Marc Shapiro, *Freddie Prinze Jr.* (New York: Berkley Publishing Group, 1999), p. 84.

## CHAPTER 6. SIZZLING SUMMERS

1. *"I Know What You Did Last Summer,"* *Reaper's Curve*, 1997, <http://www.geocities.com/reaperscurve/notes.html> (October 17, 2007).
2. "AOL Chat Transcript," *AOL*, January 27, 2001, <http://www.ilovefreddie.com/transcript_aolchat01.html> (October 28, 2007).
3. RoseEtta Stone, "Interview with Lois Duncan," *Absolute Write Newsletter*, January 18, 2002, <http://www.absolutewrite.com/specialty_writing/lois_duncan.htm> (October 17, 2007).
4. Lynn Feigenbaum, "Report to Readers R-Rated Reviews: Are We Guilty?" *The Virginian-Pilot*, University Libraries, Virginia Tech, November 2, 1997, <http://scholar.lib.vt.edu/VA-news/VA-Pilot/issues/1997/vp971102/10310023.htm> (October 24, 2007).
5. RoseEtta Stone.
6. Marlien Rentmeester, "Wait Until Dark," *Seventeen*, November 1997, p. 126.
7. "The Facts of Life," *Soap Opera Magazine*, n.d., <http://www.kimberlymccullough.net/articles1.htm> (October 28, 2007).
8. *"I Know What You Did Last Summer,"* *Box Office Mojo*, n.d., <http://www.boxofficemojo.com/movies/?id=iknowwhatyoudidlastsummer.htm> (November 3, 2007).
9. "The Rosie O'Donnell Show (transcript)," January 13, 1999, *JennaAngelfire*, <http://www.angelfire.com/me/JennaAngelfire/rosie.html> (October 29, 2007).
10. "Wing Commander," *Wing Commander: Combat Information Center*, January 31, 1999, <http://www.wcnews.com/news/update/516> (October 17, 2007).

11. David A. Keeps, "Prince Freddie," *Teen People*, June/July 2001, p. 84.

12. "I Still Know What You Did Last Summer," *The Numbers*, n.d., <http://www.the-numbers.com/movies/1998/ IKNO2.php> (November 3, 2007).

## CHAPTER 7. HITS AND MISSES

1. "Freddie Prinze," *AOL's Entertainment Asylum Transcript* (online chat), *JennaAngelfire*, March 11, 1999, <http:// www.angelfire.com/mi/JennaAngelfire/aolasly.html> (October 26, 2007).

2. "Chat with Rachael Leigh Cook!" *CosmoGIRL!*, August 10, 2000, <http://rachaelleighcook.net/news/2000.08.10.00. shtml> (October 28, 2007).

3. "The 50 Most Beautiful People in the World 2000: Freddie Prinze Jr. Actor," *People Weekly*, May 8, 2000, p. 102.

4. "AOL Chat Transcript," *AOL*, January 27, 2001, <http:// www.ilovefreddie.com/transcript_aolchat01.html> (October 28, 2007).

5. "The 50 Most Beautiful People in the World 1999— Freddie Prinze Jr.," *People*, May 10, 1999, p. 197.

6. Eric Deggans, "Freddie Prinze, Jr.," *Hispanic*, September 2005, p. 16.

7. "The Tonight Show With Jay Leno (transcript)," *JennaAngelfire*, December 7, 1998, <http://www. angelfire.com/me/JennaAngelfire/TonightShow.html> (October 28, 2007).

8. "AOL Chat Transcript."

9. Marc Shapiro, *Freddie Prinze Jr.* (New York: Berkley Publishing Group, 1999), p. 133.

10. Mike Szymanski, "Freddie Prinze Jr. Talks about 'Summer Catch' and Baseball," *Zap2It.com*, August 24, 2001, <http://movies.zap2it.com/movies/features/profiles/ story/0,1259,---8299,00.html> (October 28, 2007).

11. "Film Hunk Prinze Jr. Eager to Slow Down," *BBC News Online-Entertainment*, January 25, 2000, <http://news.bbc.co.uk/1/hi/entertainment/618235.stm> (October 28, 2007).

12. Ellen A. Kim, "Brandy Denies Addiction Rumors," *Newsmakers: Hollywood.com*, January 22, 2000, <http://www.hollywood.com/news/NEWSMAKERS_Brandy_denies_addiction_rumors/311878> (November 3, 2007).

13. David A. Keeps, "Prince Freddie," *Teen People*, June/July 2001, p. 84.

## CHAPTER 8. MOVING ON

1. Michelle Tauber, et. al., "Viva el Amour!" *People*, September 30, 2002, p. 56.

2. "Why Freddie Prinze, Jr. Has Quit the Big Screen for TV," *The TV Tattler—AOL Television*, February 7, 2006, <http://television.aol.com/news/tv_tattler_celebrity_interviews/freddie_prinze> (October 28, 2007).

3. Clarissa Cruz, "The Prinze and the Slayer," *Entertainment Weekly*, June 2002, <http://www.ew.com/ew/article/0,,262333,00.html> (October 28, 2007).

4. Clarissa Cruz, "A Prinze, a Slayer & a Dog Named Doo," *Entertainment Weekly*, June 21, 2002, <http://www.ew.com/ew/article/0,,262690_4,00.html> (October 28, 2007).

5. Ibid.

6. Sherri Sylvester, "Prinze Plays Himself in 'Down to You,'" *CNN Entertainment News*, January 20, 2000, <http://archives.cnn.com/2000/SHOWBIZ/Movies/01/20/down.to.you/index.html> (November 3, 2007).

7. "The 50 Most Beautiful People in the World 2000: Freddie Prinze Jr. Actor," *People Weekly*, May 8, 2000, p. 102.

8. Liane Bonin, "'Boys' to Men," *EW.COM (Entertainment Weekly)*, June 20, 2000, <http://www.ew.com/ew/report/

0,6115,85298_1%7C14112%7C%7C0_0_,00.html>
(October 28, 2007).

9. "Freddie Prinze Jr. Pays a Visit to the Orthodontist," *The Internet Movie Database (IMDb)*, June 15, 2000, <http://www.imdb.com/title/tt0204175/news> (October 28, 2007).

10. Ellen A. Kim, "Prinze of Hearts," *Hollywood.com*, June 3, 2000, <http://p070.ezboard.com/ffreddieprinzejr8733freddienews.showMessage?topicID=59.topic> (October 28, 2007).

11. "Freddie Prinze Jr. Gets Unwanted Female Attention," *The Internet Movie Database (IMDb)*, February 1, 2001, <http://www.imdb.com/title/tt0192111/news> (October 28, 2007).

12. "The 50 Most Beautiful People in the World 2000: Freddie Prinze Jr. Actor."

13. Clarissa Cruz, "The Prinze and the Slayer."

14. Jamie Russell, "Freddie Prinze Jr., Scooby-Doo," *BBC*, July 1, 2002, <http://www.bbc.co.uk/films/2002/07/01/freddie_prinze_jr_scooby_doo_interview.shtml> (November 2, 2007).

15. Bonnie Churchill, "Teen Idol is Always Ready to Step Up to the Plate," *Christian Science Monitor*, August 31, 2001, p. 18.

## CHAPTER 9. ROMANCE, DOGS, AND BASEBALL

1. Clarissa Cruz, "A Prinze, a Slayer & a Dog Named Doo," *Entertainment Weekly*, June 21, 2002, <http://www.ew.com/ew/article/0,,262690,00.html> (October 28, 2007).

2. John Griffiths, "Sarah Rides a Heat Wave," *Cosmopolitan*, August 1, 2002, p. 184.

3. Sean Daly, "Co-stars Prinze and Gellar Get Ready to Say I Scooby-Do," *Toronto Star*, June 12, 2002, p. F02.

4. Griffiths, p. 184.

5. Greg Adkins, et. al., "Freddie Prinze, Jr.," *People*, December 27, 2004, p. 30.

6. Deborah Baer, "Prinze Charming," *CosmoGIRL!*, September 2001, p. 124.

7. "Freddie Prinze Jr. Helps To Break-in Inexperienced Actress," *The Internet Movie Database (IMDb)*, July 27, 2001, <http://imdb.com/title/tt0234829/news> (October 28, 2007).

8. David A. Keeps, "Prince Freddie," *Teen People*, June/July 2001, p. 84.

9. Todd Gold, "Steady Freddie," *Rollingstone.com*, August 23, 2001, <http://www.rollingstone.com/news/story/5932918/steady_freddie> (October 28, 2007).

10. Mike Szymanski, "Freddie Prinze Jr. Talks about '*Summer Catch*' and Baseball," *Zap2It.com*, August 24, 2001, <http://movies.zap2it.com/movies/features/profiles/story/0,1259,---8299,00.html> (October 28, 2007).

11. Keeps, p. 84.

12. Baer, p. 124.

13. "*Scooby-Doo*," *Box Office Mojo*, n.d., <http://www.boxofficemojo.com/movies/?id=scoobydoo.htm>, (November 3, 2007).

14. Paul Fischer, "The Prinze Catches Some Summer Fun," Interview: *A List Star*, <http://www.dealmemo.com/Interview/Freddy_Prinze_Jnr.htm> (November 3, 2007).

15. Jeff Jensen, Sarah Michelle Gellar, et. al., "The Goodbye Girl," *Entertainment Weekly*, March 7, 2003, <http://www.ew.com/ew/article/0,,427434_3,00.html> (November 3, 2007).

16. Ibid.

17. "Gellar's McDonalds Ban," *World Entertainment News Network*, April 21, 2004, <http://www.imdb.com/news/wenn/2004-04-21> (November 2, 2007).

18. "Sarah Michelle Gellar's Wedding to Get Hollywood Direction," *The Internet Movie Database (IMDb)*,

February 6, 2002, <http://www.imdb.com/name/
nm0005327/news> (November 3, 2007).

19. Michelle Tauber, et. al., "Viva el Amour!" *People*,
September 30, 2002, p. 56.

20. Jensen, "The Goodbye Girl."


CHAPTER 10. BRANCHING OUT

1. Bryon Gordon, "They Told My Mom I Was Schizo,"
*Telegraph (London)*, January 2003, <http://www.
freddieprinzejr.com/articles_tele03.htm> (October 28,
2007).

2. "Answer the Questions! Freddie Prinze Jr.; I am my Own
Male Role Model," *The Independent on Sunday*, (London),
February 9, 2003, <http://www.findarticles.com/p/
articles/mi_qn4159/is_20030209/ai_n12734673/print>
(October 28, 2007).

3. "*Scooby-Doo 2: Monsters Unleashed*," Box Office Mojo,
n.d., <http://www.boxofficemojo.com/movies/?id=
scoobydoo2.htm> (November 6, 2007).

4. Kate O'Hare, "Freddie Prinze Jr. Refuses to be Limited,"
*Zap2it.com*, April 16, 2003, <http://tv.zap2it.com/
tveditorial/tve_main/1,1002,271%7C81079%7C1%7C,
00.html> (October 28, 2007).

5. "Freddie Prinze Jr. Writes *Mutant X*," *Comics Continuum*,
February 4, 2003, <http://www.comicscontinuum.com/
stories/0302/04/index.htm> (October 28, 2007).

6. Chris Strauss and Mark Dagostino, "Proud Prinze,"
*People*, October 31, 2005, p. 125.

7. "The Late Freddie Prinze Gets Hollywood Star,"
*Associated Press*, December 15, 2004, <http://www.
usatoday.com/life/people/2004-12-15-prinze-star_x.
htm> (October 28, 2007).

8. "Integrity. Sweetness. Smoldering Good Looks. Family
Loyalty. And He Cooks a Mean Pork Chop," *Redbook*,
September 2005, p. 47.

9. Eric Deggans, "Freddie Prinze, Jr.," *Hispanic*, September 2005, p. 20.
10. John Crook, "Freddie Prinze Savors Tough Demands," *Zap2it.com*, October 30, 2005, <http://movies.msn.com/tv/article.aspx?news=205753> (October 28, 2007).
11. Ibid.
12. Bridget Byrne, "Paternal Instinct: Freddie Prinze Jr. Takes Sitcom Duties Seriously," *The Record*, February 15, 2006, p. F05.
13. "AOL and Warner Bros. Launch In2TV—the First Broadband Television Network." *Time Warner*, March 15, 2006, <http://www.timewarner.com/corp/newsroom/pr/0,20812,1173404,00.html> (October 28, 2007).
14. Ibid.
15. "Gellar Turned Down 'Stardust' Role for Love," *World Entertainment News Network*, August 3, 2007, <http://www.imdb.com/name/nm0005327/news> (November 3, 2007).
16. "Integrity. Sweetness. Smoldering Good Looks. Family Loyalty. And He Cooks a Mean Pork Chop," p. 47.
17. John Griffiths, "Sarah Rides a Heat Wave," *Cosmopolitan*, August 1, 2002, p. 184.

# Further Reading

Abrams, Lea. *Freddie Prinze*. Philadelphia: Chelsea House, 2002.

Belli, Mary Lou, and Dinah Lenney. *Acting for Young Actors: The Ultimate Teen Guide*. New York: Back Stage Books, 2006.

Castro, Iván A. *100 Hispanics You Should Know*. Westport, Conn.: Libraries Unlimited, 2007.

Jordan, Victoria. *Freddie Prinze, Jr*. New York: Pocket Books, 2000.

Lopez, Jose Javier. *Puerto Rico*. Philadelphia: Chelsea House Pub., 2006.

MacDonald, Elizabeth. *Sarah Michelle Gellar*. London: Carlton Books, 2002.

Mason, Paul. *Sarah Michelle Gellar*. Chicago: Raintree, 2005.

McCracken, Kristin. *Freddie Prinze, Jr*. New York: Children's Press, 2000.

Mintzer, Richard. *Latino Americans in Sports, Film, Music, and Government: Trailblazers*. Philadelphia: Mason Crest Publishers, 2006.

O'Brien, Lisa. *Lights, Camera, Action!: Making Movies and TV From the Inside Out*. Toronto: Maple Tree Press, 2007.

Otfinoski, Steven. *Latinos in the Arts*. New York: Facts on File, 2007.

Rivera, Ursula. *Rachael Leigh Cook*. New York: Children's Press, 2002.

Wilson, Wayne. *Freddie Prinze, Jr*. Bear, Del.: M. Lane, 2001.

# Internet Addresses

Freddie Prinze, Jr.
  <http://www.freddieprinzejr.com>
  *A fan site with links to articles and photographs.*

I Love Freddie—Freddie Prinze, Jr., Fan Site
  <http://www.ilovefreddie.com/>

# Index